BATTLES
in the
PROMISED LAND

BATTLES
in the
PROMISED LAND

*Suffering, Hope,
and the Abundant Christian Life*

JACOB HAYWOOD

Foreword by Brandon Heath

Illustrations by George Scondras

WIPF & STOCK · Eugene, Oregon

BATTLES IN THE PROMISED LAND
Suffering, Hope, and the Abundant Christian Life

Copyright © 2024 Jacob Haywood. All rights reserved. Except for brief quotations in critical publications or reviews, no part of this book may be reproduced in any manner without prior written permission from the publisher. Write: Permissions, Wipf and Stock Publishers, 199 W. 8th Ave., Suite 3, Eugene, OR 97401.

Wipf & Stock
An Imprint of Wipf and Stock Publishers
199 W. 8th Ave., Suite 3
Eugene, OR 97401

www.wipfandstock.com

PAPERBACK ISBN: 978-1-6667-6388-1
HARDCOVER ISBN: 978-1-6667-6389-8
EBOOK ISBN: 978-1-6667-6390-4

VERSION NUMBER 020624

Now I Lay Me Down to Fight by Katy Bowser Hutson. Copyright © 2023 by Katherine Jane Hutson. Used by permission of InterVarsity Press, P.O. Box 1400, Downers Grove, IL 60515, USA. www.ivpress.com

The ESV® Bible (The Holy Bible, English Standard Version®). ESV® Text Edition: 2016. Copyright © 2001 by Crossway, a publishing ministry of Good News Publishers. The ESV® text has been reproduced in cooperation with and by permission of Good News Publishers. Unauthorized reproduction of this publication is prohibited. All rights reserved.

For Jaimie

Contents

Foreword by Brandon Heath | ix
Preface | xi

PART ONE—JOSHUA
Suffering as Part of the Abundant Christian Life

CHAPTER ONE
Preparing for the Promised Land: The Battle of Submission | 3

CHAPTER TWO
Trusting the Planner Over the Plan: The Battle of Faith | 9

CHAPTER THREE
Recalling God's Past Faithfulness: The Battle of Remembering | 16

CHAPTER FOUR
Keeping the Law: The Battle of Obedience | 29

PART TWO—DAVID
Turning Heartaches into Hope-filled Laments

CHAPTER FIVE
Learning to Lament: The Battle of Desperation | 39

CHAPTER SIX
Giving Thanks in All Circumstances: The Battle of Gratitude | 49

CHAPTER SEVEN
Pairing Laments with Praise: The Battle of Worship | 57

CHAPTER EIGHT
Connecting Through Real-Life Laments: The Battle of Honest Expression | 67

PART THREE—JESUS THE SUFFERING SERVANT
Our Position in God's Grand Redemptive Story

CHAPTER NINE
Recognizing He is Enough: The Battle of Expectations | 89

CHAPTER TEN
Overcoming Your Lineage: The Battle of Legacy | 98

CHAPTER ELEVEN
Living in the Already/Not Yet: The Battle of Redemption | 107

CHAPTER TWELVE
Trusting in the Empty Tomb: The Battle of Living Again | 117

PART FOUR—JESUS THE CONQUERING KING
The Final End of Suffering and Hope

CHAPTER THIRTEEN
Fighting a Kingdom You Cannot See: The Battle of Spiritual Warfare | 129

CHAPTER FOURTEEN
Celebrating His Second Coming: The Battle of Waiting | 140

CHAPTER FIFTEEN
Pressing On with Forever in Mind: The Battle of Hope | 148

CHAPTER SIXTEEN
Comprehending the Greatest of Loves: The Battle is No More | 154

Bibliography | 165

Foreword

I REMEMBER THE FIRST time I visited the Holy Land. It was a place I had read about many times in the Bible, and I never imagined I might one day set foot where Jesus and his disciples walked. The first few days of our trip were spent in what our highly educated tour guide referred to as "The Galilee." I had read about and knew of course Nazareth was a Galilean town, but putting a "the" in front of it was new for me. The Galilee is actually a region of lush green, beautiful hills and valleys, dotted with small settlements and farms and a few small cities. It's not the dry, arid landscape I imagined of Jerusalem or the Dead Sea. It kind of reminded me of the foothills of the Appalachians. We peaked one of the largest hills, maybe even a mountain, overlooking what is referred to as The Valley of Armageddon. It is apparently the future sight of a great battle to come where all things will end. We looked down on this honestly gorgeous valley with both awe and terror. Our tour guide said, and I'm trusting her on this, that Napoleon Bonaparte himself visited the site and agreed it was the perfect stage for a battlefield.

What Jacob has done with this book is remind us that this Promised Land, this place that was prepared for us, is anything but safe. Nor is it permanent. These wonderfully complex and resilient bodies God has given us are not without frailty or pain. And while this life is a gift, it comes with great conflict.

I have known Jacob since he was kid. I was a kid myself, having inherited his family by way of my father and his aunt being married. I watched he and his twin sister Jaimie grow up, and I was with him when he eulogized her at her untimely death. If someone is going to speak of battles, you want to hear it from someone who has climbed from the trenches. Someone who has some scars and perspective. Jacob not only bears those wounds, but he has wisdom of the Scripture and is a pastor. It's humbling to see a guy that

FOREWORD

I knew as a five year old, grow into a man I now look to for wisdom and guidance.

I pray that this book will open your eyes to see that even through the challenges you face, God is making a way. And the most perfect and complete way he made cost him his only son.

Brandon Heath

Preface

Pain. Loss. Hardship. Suffering. These are words no one likes to hear or dwell on, but their reality is inevitable in this life. Everyone has a story of suffering. Everyone's suffering is different. Everyone's suffering matters.

Maybe your story of suffering is hearing the words, "The cancer has spread," or trying to find energy to attend to your special needs child every day. Maybe it's taking care of your aging and stubborn parent who doesn't recognize you or being denied once again from the dream job you wish you could land. Maybe it's fighting for your marriage when it would be easier to throw in the towel or praying for years to have children when all your friends have completed their families by now. Whatever your struggle, we have all experienced suffering and will continue to face it in different forms the longer we live.

No matter how hard we might try to avoid suffering, we won't. It's part of being human and living in an imperfect world. It's also an integral part of the Christian life, as Jesus told his followers they would face.[1] So why as Christians are we often surprised when we go through hard times? Like everyone else, we know we will suffer, but we often operate under the false expectation that those who truly follow Jesus should be exempt. After all, hasn't God promised his followers an abundant life?[2] Yes, he has. But what if God's means of blessing was through *suffering*? Would you choose that path?

It seems like an oxymoron—blessing through suffering—but in reality, it is the biblical standard.

When looking through the lens of faith guided by the words of the sufferers gone before us, it is evident that suffering leads to God's glory

---

1. John 16:33.
2. John 10:10.

and our good (not that it always *feels* good). This imagery is clear in the book of Joshua when the Israelites finally make it to the Promised Land and then experience one battle after another. The path was not easy, but it was worth traversing, not only for Joshua and the Israelites, but also for us today. Sometimes God takes us on a path that is long, dark, and winding, but it is a path we never have to travel alone—there is always a Light and a Guide. No amount of willpower or strength can reach the end of the path of suffering, but there is a Mighty One on whose wings we will fly when we have no strength left to crawl.[3] And once the end is reached, the sufferer can receive peace and rest if in Christ.

The end I'm referring to here in this book is not heaven, even though many people often use "heaven" and "Promised Land" synonymously. The Promised Land in the Bible refers to the abundant Christian life here on earth. One way we know this is true is because Revelation reveals that there are no more battles in heaven. The great Bible commentator, J. Vernon McGee explains it like this:

> The Promised Land cannot be a type of heaven since heaven is not a place of conflict and conquest. Heaven is received as a gift of the grace of God. Rather, the Promised Land represents the place to which believers are brought right here in this world today.[4]

Though there are no battles in heaven, there were many battles Joshua, David, and even Jesus fought while in their earthly Promised Land. And there are undoubtedly battles we will fight as well amidst the abundant Christian life promised to us here and now.

My battle of suffering commenced on April 4, 2014 and still continues to this day when my twin sister, Jaimie, unexpectedly died at twenty-six years of age. She was a dedicated mother of two small children, a beloved wife, a joyful daughter, and not just my sister but one of my very best friends. She was a devout follower of Jesus, too, and we prayed and believed God would heal her sudden sickness. Yet he didn't answer the way we hoped. The moment she took her last breath, her faith was realized and mine was tested like never before.

I don't know why it was part of God's plan for my twin sister to leave this earth so soon. I don't know why children get cancer. I don't know why God allows natural disasters, poverty, disease, and war to rip apart families

---

3. Isa 40:31.
4. McGee, *Joshua and Judges*, x.

and nations. I don't know why bad things happen to good people. I don't know why there is so much pain and suffering in this world. I don't know why . . . I don't know why . . . I don't know why. But in the days, weeks, and years following my sister's death, I have learned that I don't have to know why, because I know God. I know he is good even when my situation screams the opposite. I know he is with me even when I can't feel him, for he promises to never leave me nor forsake me. I know his plans will prevail for my ultimate good and his ultimate glory, even if they are different from what I expected. I know that I can trust him because even through the hardest suffering, I have learned there is hope. And that is what I want you to learn through this book. There are battles in the Promised Land, but you can still have abundance of life amidst them.

Through my personal story of suffering the loss of my twin sister in the prime of her life and through biblical examples of how Joshua, David, and Jesus also suffered in the Promised Land, this book will outline how God is faithful amidst our suffering and how, even through hardship, the abundant Christian life is still possible.

No matter where you are in your journey of suffering, know this: God is fighting with you in your battle—going before you, standing in front of you, and guarding behind you. There are going to be battles in your Promised Land, but you can still have abundance of life. Are you ready to embrace this journey? Let's go!

PART ONE

JOSHUA

Suffering as Part of the Abundant Christian Life

Chapter One

Preparing for the Promised Land
The Battle of Submission

Joshua 1:2–5

²"Moses my servant is dead. Now therefore arise, go over this Jordan, you and all this people, into the land that I am giving to them, to the people of Israel. ³ Every place that the sole of your foot will tread upon I have given to you, just as I promised to Moses. ⁴ From the wilderness and this Lebanon as far as the great river, the river Euphrates, all the land of the Hittites to the Great Sea toward the going down of the sun shall be your territory. ⁵ No man shall be able to stand before you all the days of your life. Just as I was with Moses, so I will be with you. I will not leave you or forsake you.

ARE YOU A GLASS-HALF-FULL or glass-half-empty type person? I am typically a glass-half-full, but my wife would say she's just a half glass. She likes to call herself a realist, meaning somewhere in the middle of a pessimist and an optimist. I tend to classify her as a glass-half-empty type because she could use a little more optimism in her life, which is where I come in *(opposites do attract)*. But in all truth, she doesn't sugar coat the hard stuff,

PART ONE—JOSHUA

and neither will this book. Sorry to disappoint anyone looking for five steps to a life full of sunshine and puppies.

Reality is, the abundant Christian life is not always a happy-go-lucky walk in the park. Mondays are as much a reality as Fridays, but God is as present amidst the worst of Mondays as he is the best of Fridays. That's where hope comes in.

Many abundant Christian lives have been marked by suffering upon suffering and struggle upon struggle. I'm sure you can think of someone who has personally inspired you by how many hardships they have overcome. And just like you see through their lives and the heroes of the Bible including Joshua, David, and Jesus, this life of battles and suffering can also be a life of immense joy that gives God great glory and us great hope.

Abundance of life is only possible when God's people trust his goodness and sovereignty and surrender to his way. Take Joshua for example. After wandering in the desert for forty years, God finally gave him the charge to lead the Israelites into the Promised Land. Joshua was ready to lead because he had been willing to follow. He followed God and his appointed leader Moses through thick and thin. Forty years prior to this charge, Joshua would not have been ready for such a feat, but at some point, even amidst desert wandering, he chose surrender.

Usually it is by walking through a fiery furnace or desert land that qualities such as endurance, perseverance, patience, and obedience are developed; qualities that prepare us for a bigger work God wants to do in our lives.

Just as this book is a product of my suffering, God has shown his faithfulness even through my darkest days. He has received much glory through my earthly loss, as you will hear more about in the pages that unfold, and he has been a constant presence through a seemingly losing battle. I hope you can say the same in your struggle. And if you can't yet, hopefully you will be able to by the end of this book.

The path where God leads is often a difficult path, but it is always the path of his greatest glory. God's path most certainly requires suffering, but he most certainly gets his people through. This promised, abundant life can be yours, if only you are willing to fight for it God's way, just like Joshua did.

Following the Leader

As a child, did you ever play the game "follow the leader"? The activity is often used in classrooms to teach students to listen and obey in an interactive and fun way. One child is the leader and demonstrates an action or command, and the rest of the class mimics what they see the leader do. If you were like me, you always wanted to be the leader. It was fun to be in charge and make other people do whatever you wished (it still is!). But the game lost its flare whenever it came to following.

When I think of Joshua, I often envision him as a larger-than-life heroic leader. He was strong. He was brave. He stood fear in the face without backing down. But Joshua was only a great leader because he was first a great follower.

Joshua had played follow the leader for some forty years. He followed Moses out of bondage and slavery in Egypt. He followed him through the Red Sea. He followed him at Mount Sinai. He followed him through his people's murmuring in the face of mass miracles and provision. He followed him through the wilderness for forty, unnecessary years—a journey that was only supposed to take days. Though Joshua knew God's people could conquer the Promised Land when he first spied it out, though he trusted God when almost everyone else doubted, though he endured God's judgement alongside his people in the form of postponed blessing, Joshua still followed.

He followed God's appointed leader, and ultimately God himself, to the end.

Great leaders are first great followers. They know how to empathize with their flock because they have walked in their shoes. Great leaders stay the course and keep the faith because they are willing to trust God and go where he leads. They have learned the importance of submission. At some point in Joshua's journey, he learned to give up his will and way for God's. He learned to yield to God's power and control. He learned to submit to God's authority and timing. Only through submission could he one day receive the fullness of the Promised Land.

Although submission and blessing go hand in hand, the act of submission feels unnatural to us. We want to be in control. We want our own way. We want our own timing. We want to be like Adam and Eve and desire to know everything that God knows as if he's holding out on us. It's likely we think that if we were in control and in charge, we would never have to endure hardship, because we assume our way is always right and good. But until we learn to submit to a God who is bigger, better, and wiser than we are, our plans and desires for our lives will always fall short.

Preparing for Greater Things

When looking at Joshua's story, we usually don't dwell on the forty years of suffering he quietly endured alongside his people as they wandered the desert. If he was the one who would ultimately lead the Israelites into the Promised Land, why couldn't he have led the charge earlier and saved them forty years of hope-deferred heartache?

One explanation is that without hardship, people cannot develop the positive character traits essential to live an upright life and fully trust God. This reason for suffering is known as the soul-making theodicy. Theodicies are biblical and philosophical explanations of how God can be all-good and all-powerful while still allowing hardship and suffering in our lives and this world. We see this in Joshua's wilderness suffering.

When God's people cowered back at the glimpse of giants, God was producing bravery in Joshua. When everyone around him doubted God would keep his promise, God was producing faith in Joshua. When God's judgment was dished out on the Israelites in the form of prolonged wandering, God was producing patience in Joshua.

Joshua probably didn't realize these characteristics were being developed as he suffered, but forty years prior to the charge to lead God's people, he wouldn't have been ready without them. The great theologian Francis Schaeffer explains it like this:

> True spiritual leadership does not come from human hands but from God. No one is indispensable; yet each person is important and unique. Usually there is preparation before leadership. God taught Joshua all these things as Joshua followed Moses in the wilderness. Then, with these lessons learned, Joshua was ready to lead the people into the promised land.[1]

As was true in Joshua's life and in ours, God has a purpose for our suffering even if we can't see it at the moment. He is working all things for the good of those who love him[2] and preparing us for a bigger work that he wants to do in our lives and within our hearts.

---

1. Schaeffer, *Joshua and the Flow of Biblical History*, 34.
2. Romans 8:28.

Suffering with a Purpose

In Nancy Guthrie's book *Holding onto Hope*, written after losing two young infants, she says, "If God has allowed suffering into your life, it is for a purpose. A good purpose. A holy purpose." She later states, "Every difficulty—from the minor irritation of a broken piece of crystal to the piercing pain of a broken relationship—God has allowed every one for the singular and supreme purpose of transforming your character into the likeness of his Son."[3]

Oftentimes, we see our suffering as something to avoid or overcome. We want to quickly move past it and come out unscathed. We want to live for the better days. We want to get out of the valley and back on the mountain top. We don't want to hurt. We don't want pain. And we wouldn't choose it if it were up to us. But when we submit our will to God's and accept the suffering he has allowed, we can receive the blessing of what is being produced in us.

The task of crossing the Jordan River and leading God's people into the Promised Land—a land flowing with milk and honey but also inhabited by giants—was daunting. But because of Joshua's desert land experience, he was ready and equipped for the charge that lay ahead. Because Joshua had seen firsthand how God had provided and sustained his people through their complaining, grumbling, and lack of faith during those forty years, he knew God wouldn't fail them now. Joshua trusted God's word when God said, "I will be with you. I will not leave you or forsake you." And we can do the same.

Joshua could not have successfully claimed the Promised Land without the hardships he endured forty years prior. There is a Promised Land here on earth for you, too, and God is developing something in you through your suffering you may not yet see. While there's no way to know the full extent of all the reasons God allows his people to suffer, you can be sure that the pain you have gone through is not in vain. In the least, it is instilling qualities in you to comfort, guide, and relate to others in ways you never have before.

Since my sister's death, my suffering has developed within me characteristics that would not be present otherwise. I had always felt bad for people who had lost loved ones tragically or unexpectedly, but now I empathize and grieve and carry their burden in a way I never could before. Even

---

3. Guthrie, *Holding On to Hope*, 31, 34.

though I've felt the sting of death that Satan intended to destroy me and my family, I've also come to know more deeply the God of all comfort that Paul talks about in 2 Cor 1:5, "For as we share abundantly in Christ's sufferings, so through Christ we share abundantly in comfort too."

Just like Joshua, our hardship and suffering has a purpose. Through it we see God's grace, provision, and fighting on our behalf. We learn of his goodness and trustworthiness in ways we wouldn't have known otherwise. And we become more like him in our character and compassion towards others who are also suffering. That's what gives us hope. Hope to get through it. Hope to keep living. Hope to trust God's ways and follow his lead no matter what.

We may not see it now, but God is working the small, hard, everyday trials into something bigger for us, often preparing and qualifying us to be used in mighty ways for him. May you trust him amidst your suffering, and may you see his mighty hand prevail in the abundant, hope-filled life he has promised to those who follow him.

Will you surrender to him and allow him to use your suffering for good today?

Chapter Two

Trusting the Planner Over the Plan
The Battle of Faith

Joshua 1:6–9

⁶ Be strong and courageous, for you shall cause this people to inherit the land that I swore to their fathers to give them. ⁷ Only be strong and very courageous, being careful to do according to all the law that Moses my servant commanded you. Do not turn from it to the right hand or to the left, that you may have good success wherever you go. ⁸ This Book of the Law shall not depart from your mouth, but you shall meditate on it day and night, so that you may be careful to do according to all that is written in it. For then you will make your way prosperous, and then you will have good success. ⁹ Have I not commanded you? Be strong and courageous. Do not be frightened, and do not be dismayed, for the Lord your God is with you wherever you go.

"A BLIND MAN WALKED into a bar. . .then a table. . .then a chair." I know, I know. That's a corny dad joke. But do you ever feel like following God's plan for your life is as if you were blindly stumbling all over the place? You've likely heard the saying, "Hindsight is 20/20." When you're living in the

PART ONE—JOSHUA

midst of your life, it can feel like you're blindly walking around, but when you look back, you can see more clearly the path you have taken.

I want you to pause and think back on your life right now. Does it look like you thought it would when you were younger? Did you follow God perfectly every step of the way? Did you ever not know where God was leading? Did you always walk in obedience no matter what?

If you are reading this book, there's a good indication that you want to follow God. For true Christians, we all do. We tell God we will follow him and desire to do so. But deep inside if we're honest, we either feel like we won't be able to follow through when it comes down to it, or we just have no clue where he is leading like we're walking around blind. Or maybe we're too comfortable with where we are right now to go any further with him. So we decide we just won't go. Not in a blatant, rebellious way. But in a subtle, idle way. I know you have been there like me, because that's the pattern of the saints throughout the entire narrative of the Bible.

We see Abraham trust God enough to move from the comforts of his homeland yet stumble and fall when it came to waiting for God's promise of a son.[1] He jumped the gun by sleeping with his maidservant to try to speed up God's plan.[2] Still, God's plan prevailed. We see Jonah run from God's plan to preach to those at Nineveh and ended up being swallowed by a big fish.[3] After repenting, he finally obeyed God, and the people turned from their sins and were spared.[4] We see Moses, Elijah, David, the disciples, and just about every other person mentioned in the Bible want to follow God and yet struggle at some point in living out the details of his plan. We are no different. We can relate to their thoughts of not being good enough or their feelings of being the only one on earth who seeks God or their questioning of not seeing how it will all add up. We can understand why those in the Bible gave into temptation and doubt, because if we're honest, we've done it too.

Obeying God's Will

Obedience is hard to learn. For those who have children, we know this by how hard it is to teach. *(And if you have mastered it, I could use some tips*

1. Gen 15:1–6.
2. Gen 16:1–4.
3. Jonah 1.
4. Jonah 2:1–3:10.

especially if you have strong willed kids like mine and have survived). Just like my kids often want to be 'the boss' and wish they could just watch TV all day and never have to do their chores or homework, we in our pride and self-centeredness often think we can decide our own fate and future and do whatever pleases us. We want to control our world and the outcome of it. We want the good and comfortable things for ourselves, and many of us think we know the best way to acquire them. But Scripture calls us to die to our flesh and follow Christ and his will above our own.

As Christians, we are called to be obedient to God no matter what. Right at the beginning of Joshua 1, we see a command from God to "Arise, go."[5] Talking to Joshua, God is saying, your past is behind you. Moses is dead. There's a future ahead of you. *"Arise, go."* We know God calls us to walk in obedience to him. But often we get distracted by other things and miss the mark. We think that in order to be obedient, we must know God's will and every detail of it before we take that first step. Well, what *is* his will? What *is* his plan? Why doesn't he just tell us what to do in an audible voice like he did with Joshua and Moses?

Have you ever had someone give you directions or tell you their name, and then seconds later, you forget what they said? Don't you wish you had written it down? Well God has written his will down for us multiple times throughout the Bible, but usually we look right past it.

1 Thessalonians 5:18 says, "Give thanks in all circumstances; for *this is the will of God* in Christ Jesus for you" (emphasis added). And 1 Thess 4:3, "For *this is the will of God*, your sanctification: that you abstain from sexual immorality." Micah 6:8 says, "He has told you, O man, what is good; and *what does the Lord require of you* but to do justice, and to love kindness, and to walk humbly with your God?" 1 Peter 2:15 states, "For *this is the will of God*, that by doing good you should put to silence the ignorance of foolish people."

We often think, surely God's will for my life includes more than this. Surely it's more glamorous than sanctification, purity, justice, and gratitude! But God's will is that we trust and follow him even when it's difficult and even when we don't understand his ways. When seeking God's will, where do you go first? The Bible or those around you? Here's what Tony Merida says in one of his commentaries, and it was convicting for me to read:

> "Many Christians spend inordinate amounts of time and energy trying to find out God's concealed will while ignoring so much

---

5. Josh 1:2.

of his revealed will. Doesn't it make sense that he would want us to give first priority and attention to the stuff he has revealed in the pages of Scripture? Why should he tell us where we should go to college or whom we're supposed to marry if we're not at all interested in making disciples or living holy lives?"[6]

People lose sleep over wondering what God's will is while minimizing his clear will revealed in Scripture. God calls us to be obedient to his will in all things. That starts in all the small acts of obedience that are clearly stated in the Bible, such as honor your parents, love your neighbor, give your tithes to God. It will be harder to follow God's will when you can't see the way if you aren't already following his will in the areas he has clearly stated. So follow God right now in what you know to do right now, and he will direct your path. Don't worry about missing the path. Just be sure you're on the right path now, and you can be sure you won't miss it down the road. And the way we know we're on the right path now is if we are following God's will as revealed in God's Word. After all, God's Word is a lamp unto our feet and a light unto our path.[7]

Knowing the Plan

Even if we as Christians can stay focused on God's will as outlined in the scriptures above, we often still ask the question when seeking whom to marry, whether to take that job, what city to raise our family in, etc. . . ."*is this God's will for my life?"* That is the question that haunts us in the stillness of the night. That is the question we study and pour over and ask for a sign for until we find an answer. That is the question that has been screamed amidst much fervent prayer. But I believe it is the wrong question. It actually doesn't even have to be asked at all. Because behind that question, we are really wanting to know all the details of God's plan for our lives.

But knowing God's plan for your life is not a prerequisite for obedience to God.

Sometimes we get so caught up in knowing God's will and plan for our lives that we often fail to actually live for him on a daily basis. So if we don't have to know exactly what God's plan is in order to follow God's plan, where do we start? Where's the beginning of obedience? Faith.

---

6. Merida, *Exalting Jesus in Acts*, 17.
7. Ps 119:105.

It starts with faith. Yet, *where* your faith is placed matters. Is it placed in God? Or is it placed in your understanding of the plan and your circumstances?

Three times in God's initial charge to Joshua, he says the words, "Be strong and courageous."[8] At no point does God tell Joshua the details of his plan. He tells him the outcome of his plan. He tells him he can trust his plan. He tells him he will be with him in that plan. But God never tells him how the plan will unfold. Yet God gave Joshua exactly what he needed to hear in that moment—to be strong and courageous with whatever may come because God would be with him. If Joshua knew all the details of the plan—the battles, death, and destruction the Israelites would soon face in the Promised Land—he might have become overwhelmed by them. He might have even been tempted to turn around and go back to the desert right then, missing out on all the blessings that were also to come.

God's plans for us often don't add up on paper.

Think about the battle plan that God had for Joshua. God was giving them the land, but it wasn't like he was handing them a present and all they had to do was open it. No, they had to fight and wage war. But they had to do it God's way (vs. 7). The first battle they faced was at Jericho. A strong, fortified city. Schaeffer describes it as "a very strong fortress prepared to resist siege."[9] And God's battle plan was to put the musicians up front and march around the strong fortified city. Oh, and shout really loud. To Joshua and the other Israelites, this battle plan wouldn't have made sense. It probably wasn't one they had practiced and prepared years for. And to the people of Jericho, they probably looked pretty dumb and irresponsible. Schaeffer goes on to say, "Joshua did not take the city by a clever human military tactic. The strategy was the Lord's."[10]

Likewise, from the world's perspective, obeying the biblical instructions God gives us may not make sense to us sometimes. But it doesn't have to. All God is asking is for you to trust him and be obedient to what he says. Philip Keller says:

> [Joshua] has seldom been given the full credit he deserves as perhaps the greatest man of faith ever to set foot on the stage of human history. In fact, his entire brilliant career was a straightforward

---

8. Josh 1:6–9.
9. Schaeffer, *Joshua and the Flow of Biblical History*, 110.
10. Schaeffer, *Joshua and the Flow of Biblical History*, 110.

story of simply setting down one foot after another in quiet compliance with the commands of God.[11]

Keller's quote makes me think of the song *"The Next Right Thing"* that Anna sings in the movie Frozen II, which I've watched with my kids many times...and alone a few times, too (don't judge me). Not to give any spoilers, but in this scene of the movie, Anna is struggling with how to move on when the grief of losing her sister has overwhelmed her. She begins to sing about how to go on, focusing on just one step at a time, doing the next right thing. The lyrics to the song are similar to what Elisabeth Elliot says strengthened her through the loss of her husband Jim. It may have even originated from the same legend. Elliot says:

> There's an old legend, I'm told, inscribed in a parsonage in England somewhere on the sea coast, a Saxon legend that said, "Do the next thing." I don't know any simpler formula for peace, for relief from stress and anxiety than that very practical, very down-to-earth word of wisdom. Do the next thing. That has gotten me through more agonies than anything else I could recommend.[12]

I think this is very applicable to how we should look at following Christ and his will daily, even and especially through suffering. Sometimes the greatest leap of faith for us is one little step. And then another. And then another. It's easy get overwhelmed by the magnitude of our grief or hurt or the mountain God is calling us to climb. It seems too much to bear when we look at all we must suffer and go through. But when we break it down to one step, the next step, it is more doable. We don't have to worry about how we will get to the end of the road. All that matters right now is that next step of obedience. "Do the next thing."

Evaluating Your Faith

For each of us, the first step we need to make is coming to Jesus and surrendering our will and way to him. It starts with faith. What is your faith in? Is it in a plan, or is it in the Planner? Knowing God's plan does not always help our obedience. Knowing God, however, does. Proverbs 3:5–6 says, "Trust in the Lord with all your heart, and do not lean on *your* own understanding. In all your ways acknowledge him, and he will make straight your paths."

---

11. Keller, *Joshua: Man of Fearless Faith*, 178.
12. Elliot, *Suffering Is Never for Nothing*, 45.

TRUSTING THE PLANNER OVER THE PLAN

So many people place their faith in a plan, sometimes even God's plan. But the object of our faith should not be in a plan. It should be in the Planner. When your faith is in a plan and the details of that plan go awry, faith deteriorates. Nights become long. Worry and fear weaken your resolve to go on, let alone stick to the plan. And when something happens that supposedly doesn't line up with our expectations of this plan, we are left disappointed. We begin to question our faith. We blame God. And often we stop obeying him altogether, assuming we misinterpreted his direction from the start. But when our faith is in the Planner, it doesn't matter what the plan is. It doesn't matter where you go or which route you take. It doesn't matter how many twists and turns there are or what happens to you or around you. You trust the One who is in charge and in control to guide you through each step.

Joshua lived this out. It didn't matter what the plan was. He knew that he needed to follow God's ways, not his own. Are you following your own way, or are you seeking and trusting God's ways with each step you take?

Joshua knew he could trust whatever God's plan was because of these words: "the Lord your God is with you wherever you go" (vs. 9). It didn't matter where they went or what they did. God was on their side. Joshua trusted him, and so can you.

Losing my twin sister in her prime of life wasn't a part of my plan. And you are likely dealing with things that weren't part of your plan either. But you can trust the Planner. You don't have to know God's plan for your life right now. You may never know it fully, and that's okay. God wants you to trust him first regardless of the plan. He calls you to obedience, and as James Montgomery Boice says regarding Joshua and our lives, "Obedience is the key to victory in God's service."[13] There is no victory without obedience. There is no obedience without trust and surrender. And you can trust God because he has proven himself to be trustworthy in the good times and the bad.

---

13. Boice, *Joshua*, 12.

Chapter Three

Recalling God's Past Faithfulness
The Battle of Remembering

Joshua 4:1–8

¹ "When all the nation had finished passing over the Jordan, the Lord said to Joshua, ² "Take twelve men from the people, from each tribe a man, ³ and command them, saying, 'Take twelve stones from here out of the midst of the Jordan, from the very place where the priests' feet stood firmly, and bring them over with you and lay them down in the place where you lodge tonight.'" ⁴ Then Joshua called the twelve men from the people of Israel, whom he had appointed, a man from each tribe. ⁵ And Joshua said to them, "Pass on before the ark of the Lord your God into the midst of the Jordan, and take up each of you a stone upon his shoulder, according to the number of the tribes of the people of Israel, ⁶ that this may be a sign among you. When your children ask in time to come, 'What do those stones mean to you?' ⁷ then you shall tell them that the waters of the Jordan were cut off before the ark of the covenant of the Lord. When it passed over the Jordan, the waters of the Jordan were cut off. So these stones shall be to the people of Israel a memorial forever." ⁸ And the people of Israel did just as Joshua commanded and took up twelve stones out of the midst of the Jordan, according to the number of the tribes of the people of Israel, just as the Lord told Joshua.

RECALLING GOD'S PAST FAITHFULNESS

Do you ever forget important things? I do. In fact, I was just about to write something revolutionary, brilliant, and life-changing, but I forgot what I was going to write. Oh well. Really though, even the best minds tend to forget. In the Sherlock Holmes book *A Study in Scarlet*, Sherlock is laughed at by his partner John Watson for forgetting that the earth revolves around the sun. Listen to their conversation:

> "That any civilized human being in this nineteenth century should not be aware that the earth travelled round the sun appeared to be to me such an extraordinary fact that I could hardly realize it."
>
> "You appear to be astonished," he said, smiling at my expression of surprise. "Now that I do know it I shall do my best to forget it."
>
> "To forget it!"
>
> "You see," he explained, "I consider that a man's brain originally is like a little empty attic, and you have to stock it with such furniture as you choose…"
>
> "But the Solar System!" I protested.
>
> "What the deuce is it to me?" he interrupted impatiently; "you say that we go round the sun. If we went round the moon it would not make a pennyworth of difference to me or to my work."[1]

Sherlock remembers so much with his incredibly deductive mind that anything deemed irrelevant to him is unnecessary for remembering. Hence, one of the greatest minds ever created (by Sir Arthur Conan Doyle) has forgotten something as basic as the earth revolving around the sun.

So why am I talking about Sherlock Holmes, and why does this matter? First off, I love Sherlock Holmes. But second, Sherlock's blunder in forgetfulness of something that is not hard to remember and something that is of great importance points to our forgetfulness of something that is not hard to remember and something that is of far greater importance. We often tend to forget God's faithfulness.

When storms come, it's easy to forget the sun. The darkness of the rain-saturated clouds hides the extraordinarily bright energizer and sustainer of this precious thing we call life. When a storm comes, we don't think of all the previous days of beautiful weather. We could be munching on an apple while sullenly staring out the window watching the downpour of cats and dogs, forgetting that all the previous days of sunlight are what provided the very apple that is currently satisfying our hunger. Actually, the

---

1. Doyle, *Study in Scarlet*, ch. II.

sunlight *and* the rain together provided the needed nutrients—but that's another analogy for another time! What I'm trying to get at, and what I think you will agree with me on, is that when trials come, all we tend to see is the trial, the storm, the rain cloud. And often amidst those trials, we tend to forget God's gracious hand that has always led us before and will lead us now.

The Israelites were the same way. They traveled for forty years in the wilderness, grumbling against the gracious God who led them out of bondage and slavery in Egypt, who provided manna from heaven to fill their stomachs every day, and who kept their clothes and shoes from wearing out for decades. Sure, they were in the desert, but they were free, and they were full. Had they remembered God's faithful hand of provision instead of only looking through the lens of their current situation, grumbling might not have even been a category in their thinking. But when they reached the edge of the Promised Land, we see them finally acknowledge God's faithfulness as they looked back and remembered.

Looking Back Fuels our Faith

God, in the way only he does by his grace commanding us for our betterment, commanded Joshua to set up twelve memorial stones as he crossed the Jordan into the Promised Land. God knew that his people were prone to forget. He knew the battles that lay ahead of them, and he knew they needed to be reminded of his victory. They had finally reached their destination, but it was God who had gotten them there. He led them through every obstacle every time, never abandoning them even though they were ungrateful, and it was by his hand that his promises had come true. If they forgot this monumental moment now, they would never persevere through the battles that certainly lay ahead—the battles that God knew they could win if they trusted and obeyed him.

As God commanded Joshua to set up stones of remembrance, something incredible happened. They remembered. If we are too quick in reading this story, we often miss this part because it sounds repetitive from the verses before. But see if you notice a difference in what Joshua says the second time he states what the stones are for:

> [19] The people came up out of the Jordan on the tenth day of the first month, and they encamped at Gilgal on the east border of Jericho. [20] And those twelve stones, which they took out of the

Jordan, Joshua set up at Gilgal. [21] And he said to the people of Israel, "When your children ask their fathers in times to come, 'What do these stones mean?' [22] then you shall let your children know, 'Israel passed over this Jordan on dry ground.' [23] For the Lord your God dried up the waters of the Jordan for you until you passed over, as the Lord your God did to the Red Sea, which he dried up for us until we passed over, [24] so that all the peoples of the earth may know that the hand of the Lord is mighty, that you may fear the Lord your God forever.[2]

This time when asked what the stones of remembrance were for, Joshua not only states how God is currently delivering them by parting the Jordan River, but he recalls how forty years ago God delivered them from the Egyptians by parting the Red Sea. Joshua's acknowledgement of God's present activity caused him to remember God's active involvement in his past. Maybe this is part of the reason God decided to part the Jordan River, to engage Joshua's memory and remind him that just as he promised to be with Moses, so also he would be with him.

The greatest miracle Moses ever performed, in regards to what has been remembered and repeated for the longest amount of time, is the parting of the Red Sea. But when trials and exhaustion from desert wanderings came, the people of God soon forgot that grand miracle. Part of the reason they forgot is because they had no mechanism of remembering. They had no external memory booster. They relied on their fallen minds, which were corrupted by their fallen hearts.

When the Israelites finally get to the edge of the Promised Land, God did not want his people to fall into the same patterns of amnesia again. So God told Joshua to create a mechanism for remembering. One that would outlast even his life. He told him to set up memorial stones and remind all who passed by that not only had God dried up the Jordan, but God had also parted the Red Sea. God is a God of continual deliverance. He did it then. He can do it now. He will do it again.

God knows how important it is for the vitality of our lives to remember what he has done. And it was their remembering that allowed the Israelites to take hold of the land that was promised to them. It was their remembering that gave them the strength and stamina to fight courageously in the battles that lay ahead. It was their remembering that helped them know they had never been alone and would never be alone no matter what giants

2. Josh 4:19–24.

they faced. It is for our good that we remember God, because remembering God's past faithfulness fuels our present and future faith and obedience, which leads to blessing and abundance of life.

Everyone has God moments in his or her life that need remembering. Everyone has Jordan River moments that need memorial stones. But I'm pretty sure you don't want to carry around a pocket full of rocks everywhere you go. So how can you practically remember? First, you must recognize who the remembering is for. Second, you must do the work of remembering. Third, you must make your remembering visible. It's as simple as that. Yet there are innumerable, practical applications into each one. Let's take a deeper look.

Recognizing Who the Remembering is For

Remembering is first for you. It's important to remember all that God has done for you because then you can know God will do it again. Think of every pit he has ever pulled you out of, and you can know that the next pit you fall into, he will get you out *again*. Remember every provision he has graciously given you, and you can know in your times of drought, he will send rain at just the right time *again*. Recall the times you have sinned, how he was slow to anger, abounding in steadfast love and faithfulness, and by his grace, quick to forgive. So the next time you stumble, you can know his grace will be sufficient *again*. Remember those times you cried? He wept, too. When you were brokenhearted? He was near. And when your anxieties engulfed you like a wave of wildfire? His presence was all you needed to be still and know he is God. Remembering God's faithfulness strengthens our faith that he will do it again and again.

But here's the deal, remembering God's past faithfulness is not only for you. It is first for you but not primarily for you, because God's provisions in our sufferings are not just for us. They are also for all who follow behind us.

God called the Israelites to set up memorial stones so that their children would ask what those stones meant. And when their children asked, they then had a wide-open door to share about God's care, provision, deliverance, power, might, strength, sovereignty, and goodness. Your remembering is so your kids will remember, too. Your sufferings are so your children's sufferings can be a little lighter. Your fight to have faith in God's faithfulness is so your children will likewise come to have faith in God's faithfulness. This will never happen if you don't remember and if you never make your remembering visible. And even if you don't have children, there are people all around you who are watching and learning about God from how you deal with hardships.

Two days after my twin sister died, the Holy Spirit led me to a Bible passage that shows the healing power our suffering can have on those around us. I remember being numb. Emotionally numb. Mentally numb. Physically numb. Spiritually numb. I remember Sunday coming and sitting in the living room of my parents' house. We were supposed to worship. I was going to share from the Word of God. But to be honest, it's hard to worship when you're numb. It's like coming home from the dentist and trying to eat noodles. It's not easy to do. Still, we knew we should. We knew we could. So we tried. And the same Holy Spirit who is the great Comforter and near to the brokenhearted, bombarded me with this passage in 2 Cor 1:2–7:

> [2] Grace to you and peace from God our Father and the Lord Jesus Christ. [3] Blessed be the God and Father of our Lord Jesus Christ, the Father of mercies and God of all comfort, [4] who comforts us in all our affliction, so that we may be able to comfort those who are in any affliction, with the comfort with which we ourselves are comforted by God. [5] For as we share abundantly in Christ's sufferings, so through Christ we share abundantly in comfort too. [6] If we are afflicted, it is for your comfort and salvation; and if we are comforted, it is for your comfort, which you experience when you patiently endure the same sufferings that we suffer. [7] Our hope for you is unshaken, for we know that as you share in our sufferings, you will also share in our comfort.

When I read this passage, I knew there was a greater purpose to my family's sufferings and mine, even though I couldn't fully see those purposes in the moment. A day later, I witnessed my uncle receive Christ at my sister's funeral while *Amazing Grace* was playing. My dad was on the front row in front of his only daughter's casket, praying for his brother by name. I had given an invitation for any who didn't know Christ to come forward, and his brother came and gave his life to Jesus that day, along with several others in the crowd. Oh, what joy during our deepest sorrow. I knew there was a greater purpose to my sister's death, and I also knew there would be people the rest of my life that would need to hear how God can bring life through death. It was hard. I didn't understand the extent of it then. But I knew it was true. I was going to receive comfort from God, and I was to bring that comfort to others.

PART ONE—JOSHUA

You may be thinking, "My suffering is nothing like that. I have never seen anything good come out of my suffering." This leads me to a second Bible passage that comes to mind. It concludes one of the greatest chapters of the Bible, which is really a chapter of remembrance. Some call it the "Hall of Faith," similar to halls of fame, which are places to remember the glories and accomplishments of the greats that have gone before. Hebrews 11 is the "Hall of Faith" for many heroes of the Old Testament who have lived by faith and are examples to us on how we should live as well.

> [29] By faith the people crossed the Red Sea as on dry land, but the Egyptians, when they attempted to do the same, were drowned. [30] By faith the walls of Jericho fell down after they had been encircled for seven days. [31] By faith Rahab the prostitute did not perish with those who were disobedient, because she had given a friendly welcome to the spies. [32] And what more shall I say? For time would fail me to tell of Gideon, Barak, Samson, Jephthah, of David and Samuel and the prophets— [33] who through faith conquered kingdoms, enforced justice, obtained promises, stopped the mouths of lions, [34] quenched the power of fire, escaped the edge of the sword, were made strong out of weakness, became mighty in war, put foreign armies to flight.

Did you recognize Joshua's conquest in that passage and see God's provisions for the Israelites over and over? When I read this, it makes me want to stand up and shout victory in Jesus! But then the text takes a sobering turn. It ends glorifying the sufferings of several unnamed heroes. Take a look at these verses and try to discern what the suffering was for, even the suffering without seemingly any hope:

> [35] Women received back their dead by resurrection. Some were tortured, refusing to accept release, so that they might rise again to a better life. [36] Others suffered mocking and flogging, and even chains and imprisonment. [37] They were stoned, they were sawn in two, they were killed with the sword. They went about in skins of sheep and goats, destitute, afflicted, mistreated— [38] of whom the world was not worthy—wandering about in deserts and mountains, and in dens and caves of the earth. [39] And all these, though commended through their faith, did not receive what was promised, [40] since God had provided something better for us, that apart from us they should not be made perfect.

Talk about intense suffering to the extent of being sawn in two *(and you thought your suffering was bad!)*. Instead of lifting our spirits with a glimmer of hope like the verses before, this passage ends with what seems to be despair: "And all these, though commended through their faith, did not receive what was promised."

Wait, what? They suffered and never saw anything positive come from their suffering? Isn't God supposed to keep his promises? How is this hopeful?

Just like these unnamed Bible heroes, there is hope in your suffering because even if you can't see it, God is working something greater through it. That is where faith comes in.

All of Hebrews 11 is about people who were commended for their faith. And what was their faith in? God and his faithfulness—not their circumstances. Even though these sufferers never received what was promised this side of heaven, we see the outcome of their sufferings on the other side. We see that "God had provided something better for us, that apart from us they should not be made perfect." We are still reading about their sufferings and knowing that if they went through it, so can we. Their sufferings give us hope for ours. If anything, it helps us see that we are not alone. God is good and is working good even if we cannot see the good for ourselves. And he always keeps his promises, even if they aren't delivered according to our timing and expectations.

Doing The Work of Remembering

When computers first came out, whole rooms would be filled with equipment that would have the capacity of storing only megabytes worth of information. Now people can carry terabytes of information in their pockets. But the human brain is all the more remarkable. It's infinitely more complex than a computer. Some estimations say that the human brain can hold around a quadrillion bytes of data.[3]

The amount of things we remember without even trying is incredible in itself. We remember language. We remember names. We remember locations. We remember faces and places and things. We remember so much more than we remember that we remember. Our brains are incredible!

But it's not enough to know that you can remember. You must actually do it in order to fuel your present and future faith and obedience in Christ. After recognizing that remembering is first for you but then goes beyond

---

3. Interlandi, "New Estimate."

PART ONE—JOSHUA

you, you must now do the actual work of remembering. But how do you remember something?

It might not come easy, especially for those of you who are like me and have trouble remembering what you walked into a room for. Or if you are the type that goes through five names before you call your last child by their actual name. So how in the world can you remember something if you're not good at remembering?

It's easier than you think.

If you take the time to be still and you let your heart engage, you can remember. Everything that God has done for you is in your brain somewhere. Every good memory is tucked away, waiting to come out. Every bit of provision and strength that the Lord has given is ready to be accessed. It is sitting in a file somewhere in your mind ready to be opened. You need to let your heart engage, and you need to let your mind remember.

I read a book years ago called *Moonwalking with Einstein: The Art and Science of Remembering Everything* that helped me learn how to best remember things. It's a great book I highly recommend, but in short, it teaches you to picture your mind like a house, or mind palace, and every bit of information you want to hang onto going in a specific place in that house. It can be a house modeled after your current home or your childhood home or something totally new. But you have to picture each room and closet and crevice to store the information you want to remember. It utilizes both your spatial memory and visual memory, which are the two most natural forms of memory that we have. Though utilizing a mind palace is helpful for things that are hard to remember, there are some memories that naturally come flooding back to us when we aren't even trying to remember.

I'm going to be vulnerable for a little bit and share something with you I have only told a select few about out of embarrassment. But it's time for a moment of transparency. Here it goes: I have cried while eating food. Twice. Full out tears in a restaurant as I'm stuffing my mouth. The first time was while I was eating white beans at Lambert's Café on vacation. The second time was while eating turnip greens at Cracker Barrel. The tears hit me out of nowhere. And it wasn't because the food was bad. The food was great *(southern-style country cooking really is the best!)*. The first time my wife just looked at me dumbfounded. I could tell she was thinking, "Is this for real? Is he actually crying over white beans?" Yes. Yes, I was.

But here's what happened. My mind and heart snuck up on me when I was least expecting it. The white beans made me remember a familiar taste, which made me remember a familiar smell, which made me remember a familiar person who I hadn't seen in years. It reminded me of my great grandmother, the way her house would smell and her beans would taste. She was an incredible woman in so many ways. Every Thanksgiving she would cook the entire *huge* Thanksgiving meal by herself for her entire *huge* family (around seventy people) in her tiny house. And she did it all from scratch with a smile and a song. Sitting in Lambert's Cafe on a vacation date with my wife, I cried because I remembered my great grandmother and the blessing that she was and the legacy that she left. I remembered a taste and smell and person, all in a moment when I was not seeking to remember.

The turnip green tear incident happened several years later but in the same way. That time I remembered her daughter, my grandmother. She has the biggest heart of anyone I've ever known, fostering forty-eight kids alongside my grandfather and changing countless young boys' lives. Turnip greens made me remember her and made my heart well up with gratitude for God blessing me and so many others with such a saint of a woman. And I cried.

You may have found some humor in my sensitivity, but the point is, your brain and heart, working together, has the potential to remember so much more than you can ever imagine. This is what God wants us to do. He wants us to remember. He wants us to remember his kindness and love and peace and provision. He wants our hearts and minds to work together to bring forth tears of remembrance for the mighty works he has done, not just in our lives but in those who have gone before.

The busyness of life often drowns out our ability to remember. We have to keep up with appointments and chores and task lists and so many other things that we fail to remember the most important things. Well, I am asking you to pause right now. Let your heart catch up to your brain, and read through this next set of questions a little more slowly than you've read through everything else so far. While thinking through them, follow wherever your heart and mind start taking you. Grab a journal if it helps you to jot things down. You're about to attempt to take a trip to the deep places of your soul, and I hope you're ready for what you'll find. I hope you're ready to remember.

First, think about your family tree. *Who were your grandparents? What was special about them? How did they raise your parents? How did your parents meet? What led your parents to the place you were born? What led your parents to the place you were raised? What was special about your parents?*

PART ONE—JOSHUA

What do you appreciate about your upbringing? What is your best memory from childhood? What developed your character? What is your greatest blessing from childhood?

Next, take a few moments to dwell on your salvation. *How did you come to faith in Jesus? What has God saved you from? How has God used you? How has God strengthened you? How has God provided for you?* If you aren't sure of your salvation, *what have been some times that you have felt the presence of God drawing you to himself? Are you ready to make that commitment to trust and follow him?*

Then, if you are married, *how did God bring you and your spouse together? How has your spouse been used to make you more holy?* If you have kids, picture each one. *How has each one enriched your life? What have they taught you in being a parent?*

Now, think about your suffering. *What has been the hardest moment of your life? How has God shown himself faithful amidst your hardship? Is there anything good you have seen come out of it?*

Every aspect of your life has been guided by the gracious and perfect hand of God. Every second that has led to where you are now has been perfectly planned and executed by God for your good and his glory. Even your sufferings. Are you tired? Remember. Are you grieving? Remember. Are you fearful or doubting or anxious or worried? Remember. Remember who God is. Remember what God has done. Remember his goodness. Remember his grace and provision. All the times he's carried you. All the times he's come through. All the times he's sustained you.

When you sit and pause, when you let your heart catch up to your mind, you will find that this is true: God is working. Always. He never sleeps nor slumbers. He never makes mistakes. He's never late. He has always been with you. He is with you now. He will be with you tomorrow. And the next day and the next. You must remember.

Making Your Remembering Visible

Sometimes we need to set up physical memorials in our life to help us remember. It's good to look back and see how far God has brought you, because hindsight is always 20/20. We sometimes get so focused on what's ahead that we tend to forget what God has done before. And if you don't make your remembering visible, you will be quicker to forget it and therefore unable to pass on the valuable lessons learned to those who follow you, which is one of the main reasons we are called to remember.

Here are three practical ways you can make your remembering visible: (1) make your own "Hall of Faith," (2) keep a journal of everyday happenings, prayers, blessings, struggles, etc., and (3) write notes in a journaling Bible to pass on to your children one day.

Just like we talked about the Hebrews 11 "Hall of Faith," you can make your own "Hall of Faith" by literally dedicating a hall in your home to display visible representations of God's faithfulness and provision over the years. These could be pictures, letters, handprints, marriage licenses, baby dedication certificates, obituaries, house keys, etc. As you walk through the hallway each day, it will remind you of God's faithfulness through both good times and bad. In the hallway of our home, we have a plaque that my wife made after my sister's death. It has her obituary, her picture, the order of service, and dried flowers from her grave. It serves as not only a reminder of who my sister was but of God's faithfulness in sustaining me through the hardest time of my life.

Another memorial stone we have in our house is a gift my sister gave us the summer before she died. We had started the process of adopting from Ethiopia, and my sister made a print of the continent of Africa with a heart over Ethiopia and the words, "Love Makes a Family" underneath. Little did we know then that months later my sister would be gone, and four years after waiting on the list to be matched, Ethiopia would close their doors to all international adoptions. Nearly ten years after that print was made, we finally adopted our precious daughter, who is not Ethiopian or even adopted internationally like we had anticipated, but she has blessed our lives immeasurably. So we hang that image to be reminded and to remind our children that God's plans do not always look like our plans. But he is still good and faithful even through the unexpected, the waiting, and the hardships of life.

Journaling is another way to make your remembering visible. My wife has been keeping journals full of prayers, daily happenings, and Scripture verses for almost two decades. Whenever she is going through a dry patch in hearing from the Lord or feeling as if he is distant, she goes back through her journals to read the countless times God has come through for her and answered her prayers before, seeing that as he was faithful then, so he will be faithful now. One day our children and grandchildren will be able

PART ONE—JOSHUA

to read through them and see God's faithfulness and provision, too, and hopefully be inspired to trust in the same God she did.

I am not a journaler, but I am a student of the Bible, so I have purchased a beautiful journal Bible for each of my children. I am slowly working my way through each Bible and a commentary, taking notes about the text, writing specific encouragements to my child, and praying for them as I read. One day when they read this Bible for themselves, they will be able to see that I have journeyed through each Word as well. And as they read the notes, they will know they have been prayed for and have a visible demonstration of the importance of God's Word in their life. After all, God's Word is like one giant memorial stone reminding us of his goodness, trustworthiness, and faithfulness over and over again and guiding us in the steps of life.

Just like the stones at the Jordan River reminded the Israelites that God had fought for them, God was fighting for them, and God would continue to fight for them—the same God is fighting for you today and asking you to remember. He doesn't want you to be prone to melancholy. He isn't a proponent of pessimism. Depression and anxiety aren't spiritual gifts endowed by the Holy Spirit. These are three of the greatest plagues to the abundant Christian life, and at their root is forgetfulness. But remembering God and his faithfulness is one way he can deliver you from these.

Even the times of darkest depressions can lead you to bask in the brightest of lights when you remember. You don't have to look very far to see God at work in your life. But often we look past the work of God and glare only at our circumstances. When the rain falls, all we see is the darkness of the clouds overhead. But the storm cloud is not all there is. The sun is still shining, it may just be hidden by the clouds for a moment. What fuels you in the meantime, and what will fuel you in the future, is remembering all the times the sun has shined before.

Remembering what God has done in the past helps you look to your future with hope and trust in a faithful God, no matter what trials you may face. Looking back fuels our faith. And faith will lead you to obedience, which will lead to blessing and abundant life for you and those who follow you, even if you don't receive it this side of heaven.

Chapter Four

Keeping the Law
The Battle of Obedience

Joshua 1:7–8, 16–18

⁷ Only be strong and very courageous, being careful to do according to all the law that Moses my servant commanded you. Do not turn from it to the right hand or to the left, that you may have good success wherever you go. ⁸ This Book of the Law shall not depart from your mouth, but you shall meditate on it day and night, so that you may be careful to do according to all that is written in it. For then you will make your way prosperous, and then you will have good success. . . .¹⁶ And they answered Joshua, "All that you have commanded us we will do, and wherever you send us we will go. ¹⁷ Just as we obeyed Moses in all things, so we will obey you. Only may the Lord your God be with you, as he was with Moses! ¹⁸ Whoever rebels against your commandment and disobeys your words, whatever you command him, shall be put to death. Only be strong and courageous."

DID YOU EVER FEAR being disciplined by your father when you were growing up? I wasn't a terrible kid, but let's just say I got in trouble a fair amount of times. My mom could discipline me and I wouldn't bat an eye. But if ever I had done something really bad, she would say, "Go wait in your room until your father gets home." In those moments, I knew I was in trouble and would have taken her punishment over my dad's in a heartbeat. I dreaded my father finding out because I had a healthy fear of him. Finally, after what seemed like hours, I would hear loud footsteps coming down the hallway when he got home from work. I think the waiting for him to get home was worse than the actual punishment he gave me.

Later when I became a dad, my dad told me that he would stomp down the hallway on purpose to make it seem like he was mad all those years before even though he really wasn't (*most of the time*). He did it to instill that fear in me that I had done wrong. To make me realize I had disappointed him. It wasn't an unsafe fear I had of him. I know many people have father figures who did not discipline with love and would take it too far. But my father was loving and kind, even in his discipline, and therefore, I didn't want to disappoint him.

Now that I am a dad, I try to instill that same healthy fear in my children. I want them to know that I'm serious about requiring obedience from them. Yes, I want them to be able to come to me with anything, but when they disobey, they need to know there will be a consequence. And after they are punished or have something taken away from them, I make sure to tell them that I love them and am a sinner in need of grace just as they are. But if I never disciplined them, I am indirectly teaching them that it is okay to disobey authorities and God anytime they don't want to do something they are asked to do. And where will it stop in the future? How far will they go? Now if I or those authorities are not operating under God's law, such as commanding them to do something that goes against Scripture, they should not obey. But my desire is that they will learn to obey me in the little things, so that they will learn to obey God in the bigger, more important things as they grow, because obedience to God always leads to blessing, "For the Lord disciplines the one he loves."[1]

There was only one battle lost in the Promised Land under the leadership of Joshua, and that was the battle of Ai. Remember God's initial charge to Joshua? God told his people they would find success if they didn't deviate to the right or to the left from what he said. Any deviation from God's ways as revealed in God's Words would lead to defeat. Following God's commands no matter how weird they seemed at the time was the

1. Heb 12:6.

only way to ensure victory and abundance of life that that victory would purchase. God's people saw this played out in the first battle of Jericho. You would think after following that crazy plan and seeing the incredible victory of the walls falling down that the Israelites would trust God and obey the remaining details. But they didn't. Well, more specifically a single Israelite didn't. Achan was his name, and his one mistake caused defeat for the entire nation. Here's what God had commanded them and how Achan deviated from his words:

> Joshua 6:18-19—[18] But you, keep yourselves from the things devoted to destruction, lest when you have devoted them you take any of the devoted things and make the camp of Israel a thing for destruction and bring trouble upon it. [19] But all silver and gold, and every vessel of bronze and iron, are holy to the Lord; they shall go into the treasury of the Lord.
>
> Joshua 7:1—But the people of Israel broke faith in regard to the devoted things, for Achan the son of Carmi, son of Zabdi, son of Zerah, of the tribe of Judah, took some of the devoted things. And the anger of the Lord burned against the people of Israel.

The Cost of Deviating from God's Law

Joshua was oblivious to what Achan had done, and when he advanced to the small city of Ai, he assumed the Lord would bring them victory just like he had done at Jericho. But they were defeated, and Joshua cried out to God in anguish. God replied:

> Joshua 7:11-12—[11] Israel has sinned; they have transgressed my covenant that I commanded them; they have taken some of the devoted things; they have stolen and lied and put them among their own belongings. [12] Therefore the people of Israel cannot stand before their enemies. They turn their backs before their enemies, because they have become devoted for destruction. I will be with you no more, unless you destroy the devoted things from among you.

The next day Achan was brought before Joshua and confessed his sin. But it was too late. He, his family, his livestock, and his house were all destroyed because of his disobedience. What he received was the complete opposite of the Promised Land abundant life. We might see that as harsh, but God was setting the standard for the Israelites to know how serious following his Word is. The same standard exists for us as well.

Most of us have the tendency to read scripture as if we are the heroes, and anything bad that happens is nothing like we would do. We often fail to remember that Jesus died because of *our* sins, too. If we are honest with ourselves, we realize we are far more often like Achan than we are Joshua. It is natural for us to think we can sneak one in on God. When God draws a line in the sand, we see how close we can get to the line or search for a way around it altogether. We spend far too much energy trying to manage our sin rather than living in freedom. It's no wonder we often feel defeated.

The Centrality of God's Word

At this point, many could say, "Well, Joshua was in the Old Testament. We are in the New Testament. Jesus paid the price for our sins and fulfilled the law, therefore we don't have to take his Word *that* seriously anymore." It's true that for those who have placed their faith in Jesus, all of their sins are forgiven—past, present, and future. There is freedom in Christ! Jesus' death on the cross was vicarious, meaning it was in our place, on our behalf. The punishment that we deserved, Jesus paid it all. His grace for us is both amazing and scandalous. But sin still has consequences, both natural and from God. And breaking the law always results in punishment.

The apostle Paul knew he was at the forefront of those being forgiven, as he referred to himself as the chief of sinners.[2] But he said in Rom 5:20, "where sin increased, grace abounded all the more." Though our sin is great, the grace of Jesus is greater, which means that where there is more sin, there is more grace. There is a train of thought behind those who would raise the question about our sins being paid for called *antinomianism*, which means "against law" or "no law." The basis of this belief takes the truth of that verse but goes a little too far in assuming that the grace freely given by Jesus makes the law obsolete, which isn't true.

Who wouldn't want more grace? We all do! And if grace is abounding, and all sins are forgiven, why worry about sinning at all? It's true, Jesus has fulfilled the law on our behalf—yes, there's freedom! But this is where the error in many people's thinking creeps in. Sinning is not freedom as we so often think it is. Sin enslaves us. Paul anticipates this antinomian response with this passage in Romans 6:

2. 1 Tim 1:15.

> [1] What shall we say then? Are we to continue in sin that grace may abound? [2] By no means! How can we who died to sin still live in it?...[6] We know that our old self was crucified with him in order that the body of sin might be brought to nothing, so that we would no longer be enslaved to sin. [7] For one who has died has been set free from sin. [8] Now if we have died with Christ, we believe that we will also live with him. . .[10] For the death he died he died to sin, once for all, but the life he lives he lives to God. [11] So you also must consider yourselves dead to sin and alive to God in Christ Jesus.[3]

Following Jesus, his Word and his ways, is what brings freedom. It brings abundant life. And if you don't follow the map, you won't get to where you need to go.

I'm what I like to call "directionally challenged." I can and have gotten lost with a GPS, which takes skill, I know. But many people live as if the journey is the destination. I understand the sentiment. The problem with it though is that the journey only matters if you arrive at the right destination. Many people live as if the journey is the destination because they do not have a worldview to make sense of a destination outside this life. If this life is all there is, then let us "Eat drink and be merry, for tomorrow we die!" This way of living is called *moral relativism*. While antinomianism says that there is no law, moral relativism says each one of us defines the law.

Moral relativism is the law of the land today. Everyone does what is right in their own eyes. At least they say it should be the law of the land. The problem is that moral relativism is actually unlivable. Nobody really lives like everyone should do what is right in their own eyes. If you come across someone who finds ultimate fulfillment in life by plucking people's nose hairs against their will, all is well until they come towards you with tweezers. I've heard it said that if you want to shut a moral relativist up, all you have to do is punch them in the nose and say you sincerely believed it was the right thing to do. They would immediately recoil and deem the action as wrong and unfair—hence, immoral. The truth is there is a moral law written on everyone's heart, whether they believe it or not. It is not always revealed in how we act, but it is clearly seen in how we react.

Many people still claim moral relativism, though. Some of their reasoning is that they don't believe the standards of the Bible are right, that everybody does bad things, that many people are unaware of a moral law, or that simply a moral law doesn't exist. But just because someone doesn't

---

3. Rom 6:1–2, 6–8, 10–11.

follow the law, doesn't believe in the law, isn't aware of the law, disagrees with the law, or breaks the law along with everyone else, doesn't mean there is no moral law. I have heard all of these objections before about why a moral law doesn't exist, and each one can be answered simply by thinking about speed limits.

Speed limits are law. If you break that specific law, you can get pulled over and be issued a ticket. You could tell the police officer, "I don't follow that law," but it doesn't change the fact that you still broke the law and will likely get a ticket. Or imagine you say, "I don't believe there is a speed limit on that road." The police officer will tell you that you are mistaken and still probably give you a ticket. Or suppose you say, "Police officer, I was unaware the speed limit was 35 instead of 55," which may have truly been the case. But your ignorance doesn't disqualify you from getting a ticket for breaking the law. Even if you disagree with that law and believe it should be at least 55 mph instead, you still broke the law. When everyone on the interstate is going above 80 mph, and you are just going with the flow of traffic (*I won't judge, I do it, too*), does it mean that you won't get a ticket? No, because when everyone passes a police officer in the median, you see a trail of red brake lights because you know that it doesn't matter if everyone else is doing it, you could still be the one to get a ticket if you are breaking the law. So just because someone doesn't follow the law, doesn't believe in the law, isn't aware of the law, disagrees with the law, or breaks the law along with everyone else, it doesn't mean the law doesn't exist.

There is a moral law written in detail in the most translated and widely dispersed book of all time, the Bible. And the law of the Bible is not meant to restrict or hinder anyone's freedom. The law is given by the One who made us all and knows how we are to best function.

Whenever my children receive a gift that requires assembly, being the dad, I'm usually the one who has to put it together. I could assume I know how to do it without the instructions and rely on my own capacities. I might do ok, but I would never be certain, especially when I see that one screw left over at the end. I could listen to other people's opinions on how they think I should put it together, but they might not know any better than me. If I really want to be certain that the gift is assembled correctly, I must look at the manual from the manufacturer. They created it. They know how it will best function. It would be reckless and irresponsible of me to never read it.

It is the same with our lives and the Word of God. Abundance of life is found in following God's ways as stated in God's Word. If we aren't in the

Bible daily, we are prone to forget and stray, and in doing so, we are risking the abundant, Promised-Land life that could be ours. This matters for each person's life and for each person's eternity. This is why the gospel is necessary. We are all lawbreakers, but Jesus took our punishment, offering the gift of abundant life both now and forever to all who would believe. And those who keep to this law, who obey every word and do not deviate to the right or to the left, will not only find freedom from sin but abundance of life both now and through eternity.

Fighting Our Flesh

It's clear that God's Word matters, and we are not to deviate from it in order to have abundance of life. But how does all of this help the sufferer? I'm glad you asked!

There are many commands in the Bible that those who are suffering find difficult to follow. It's easy to glance over them and pretend they don't exist or aren't as important as other commands, like love your neighbor and do not murder. But if we heed these commands amidst our suffering, it will bring forth life within us and around us. Let's take 1 Thess 5:16–18 for example, since we have already mentioned this verse: "Rejoice always, pray without ceasing, give thanks in all circumstances; for this is the will of God in Christ Jesus for you."

How often does it say to rejoice? Just when things are going our way? No, always. That means you can and should fight to rejoice even in your hardships. If you do you will find that just as in remembering, you have a reason to rejoice. We must act in obedience to experience this abundance of life command, even if it's against our flesh.

How often should we pray? Only when we feel close to God? No, we are to pray without ceasing. That means you can and should go to God with anything at any time. And when you do, even if at first you feel like God is distant, you will know that he hears. And as you draw near to him, he will draw near to you.[4]

When should we give thanks? Just when we have something to be thankful for? No, in all circumstances. When we give thanks even amidst our suffering, it causes us to remember and realize that God works all things for good for those who love him.[5]

4. Jas 4:8.
5. Rom 8:28.

Following God's Word in obedience is not always easy. Most of the time it is hard because it goes against our flesh and the ways of the world. But it is always for our good, and it always leads to abundance of life, even amidst our suffering. Joshua and the Israelites would have never received the blessing of a land flowing with milk and honey if they were not obedient to God's Word. Schaeffer pointedly shows the example we must follow if we want to experience this same abundance of life: "Throughout his life, Joshua was obedient. Of all the factors that gave him such success, the most important was that he heeded God's admonition about the book. . .Joshua lived out his life in a practical way within the circle of the written revelation."[6]

The same book of God's Word is available to you today. Will you live your life within the circle of its revelation, not departing to the right or the left, and fight against your weary flesh? Remember God's past faithfulness, and walk in obedience even when you can't see the way right now. Just like a blind man has to trust the voice of the one leading him, turn and trust Jesus. Just take one step towards his voice. Then another. Until each act of obedience leads you further and further into the intricate plan and purposes God has for your life. It is worth it!

---

6. Schaeffer, *Joshua and the Flow of Biblical History*, 39.

PART TWO

DAVID
Turning Heartaches into Hope-filled Laments

Chapter Five

Learning to Lament
The Battle of Desperation

Psalm 51:3-4, 7-12

³ For I know my transgressions,
 and my sin is ever before me.
⁴ Against you, you only, have I sinned
 and done what is evil in your sight,
so that you may be justified in your words
 and blameless in your judgment.

⁷ Purge me with hyssop, and I shall be clean;
 wash me, and I shall be whiter than snow.
⁸ Let me hear joy and gladness;
 let the bones that you have broken rejoice.
⁹ Hide your face from my sins,
 and blot out all my iniquities.
¹⁰ Create in me a clean heart, O God,
 and renew a right spirit within me.
¹¹ Cast me not away from your presence,
 and take not your Holy Spirit from me.
¹² Restore to me the joy of your salvation,
 and uphold me with a willing spirit.

PART TWO—DAVID

DID YOU KNOW THAT every song that has ever been written came from the same twelve notes? I realized this simplistic complexity of all the centuries of songwriting while listening to "After All These Years" by Andrew Peterson, a modern-day Christian singer/songwriter and brilliantly poignant lyricist. Throughout the song, Peterson recollects his life and musical career, noting and embracing both the ups and the downs in his twenty plus years of songwriting:

> After all this time
> I thought the rhythms and the rhymes
> Would come so easy
> But it's still so hard
> It's the same twelve notes, six strings,
> And a million little mysteries
> And one broken heart...

What is captured in these lines is the heart of every song. Every song conveys not just a melody, but an emotion. And just like every song has recycled notes in different forms and order, so do the emotions songs seek to express. The second verse of the same song talks about the struggle of the human experience, which I definitely can relate to Peterson's confession:

> After all these years
> I would've thought that all my fears were laid to rest
> But I still get scared
> And I thought that all my struggles
> Would be victories by now, but I confess
> That the mess is there
> But oh-
> I know the work that You began
> Is coming to an end someday
> After all these years...

It's songs like these that give me the encouragement and wherewithal to keep traversing my Promised Land no matter how rocky the path gets. This song speaks to my heart, not just because of Peterson's mastery with words and imagery, but because he understands the struggle, fear, and hardship of the human experience, and he's not afraid to embrace it. He also knows the end of the story—that for those in Christ, there's always hope.

I can think of another brilliant lyricist with poetic mastery of words and melodic expertise who, like Peterson, understood the human condition and embraced it, all while seeing hope in every troubling circumstance. This person's songs have been sung more than any writer's songs of all time, and they are contained in the largest book of the Bible—Psalms. This singer and songwriter's name was David, and just like Joshua, he had to face battles in the Promised Land to experience abundance of life.

David, the writer of most of the Psalms, was king of Israel in the same Promised Land Joshua had conquered and claimed for the Israelites hundreds of years before. But Joshua was not able to conquer all of the land promised for all time. It was hundreds of years later that David would become king, fight physical and spiritual battles in the same Promised Land, and fulfill the charge God had first given to Joshua.

Despite enemies on every side, the excruciating confession of sin, broken relationships, wayward children, unfulfilled dreams, and the numbing pain of losing a child, David still lived an abundant life. David rightly understood the human condition through his own heartache, isolation, temptation, and sin. But he also demonstrated how to rightly cast his cares before the only one who could do something about them. Not only did David seek to live for God in the face of suffering, but he also recorded his thoughts and feelings through his suffering so that by God's design, you and I would be filled with hope while reading and singing them still today.

The Psalms have always been a great comfort to me, as they have been to countless sufferers ever since the words were penned. But majority of the Psalms are not happy, upbeat, "Everything is Awesome!" type songs. The majority of the Psalms are laments. To lament means to cry out. To cry out in despair. To cry out in fear. To cry out in anger, protest, and doubt. However, laments are more than despair, doubt, fear, and complaint. They are a hopeful crying out to someone who will see and hear and help. Laments are directed toward the only One who can do something about the helpless state for which you are crying, no matter the situation.

David lived to lament in the Promised Land because God first heard his people's laments in Egypt and promised them a "land flowing with milk and honey."[1] It was from a place of suffering that they cried out to God for help, and what ensued from their groanings—their laments—is "God heard," "God remembered," "God saw," "God knew."[2] Not only did God hear, but God answered. He sent Moses as a deliverer to battle with the Egyptians and lead his people to the Promised Land, which was a direct response to their laments. Around four hundred years later, David is king

---

1. Exod 3:8, 17.
2. Exod 2:24–25.

in that same milk-and-honey land, and even though he wasn't under oppression like his Hebrew forebearers, he still had to battle for the abundant life God had promised. But just as God heard the Hebrews when they cried out to him amidst their hardships, he heard David, too. And he hears you.

The Psalms are an insightful look into the heart of a man who (1) desperately sought to live for God so much so that both the Old Testament and New Testament call him "a man after God's own heart,"[3] and (2) suffered intense emotional and physical turmoil, some because of his own sin and some because of reasons outside his control. Every time David cried out to God, he was crying out for God's deliverance, for God's strength, and for God's protection. And he did it with hope.

Laments are both a confession and a call for action that should lead us towards hope. If our lament doesn't lead to hope, then it's neither beneficial nor is it actually a lament. Rather it becomes a complaint, which we know led to Israel's wandering in the desert for forty years. So how do we lament properly and put into practice this often-neglected act?

Through David's example, we learn that through confession of weakness, a directional posture towards God, asking God to act on our behalf, and placing our hope ultimately in him, we can properly and regularly lament, even when our heart aches just like David's did. Let's take a closer look at each of these four characteristics of laments so that we can put them into practice.

Confessional

Laments are inherently confessional in nature, either admitting personal failures that have led to our peril (sin), or telling God that we don't have the strength or power to continue on our own. R. C. Sproul states that "If you read Psalm 51 and read it carefully and thoughtfully, that Psalm will reveal more than anything else in the history of David why David was called a man after God's own heart. Because here it reveals the broken heart of a sinful man who sees his sin clearly."[4]

So many people feel sorry about their sin but rarely ever lament over it. But godly sorrow should lead to repentance.[5] You must first feel the weight of your sin before you are willing to ditch it. When someone confesses their

---

3. 1 Sam 13:14; Acts 13:22.
4. "Man After God's Own Heart," Ligonier Ministries.
5. 2 Cor 7:10.

waywardness with tears, not just fears, is when heart transformation can happen. When we truly consider the cost of our sins, it should naturally lead to godly, sorrowful confession. After all, it was for your sin that the perfect, Holy One was crushed.

The God who breathed out stars and exists outside of time and space entered time and space on a little blue planet circling a single star because of your sin. But he didn't come to crush you. He didn't come to wag his finger at you. He didn't come in power to wipe away all the sinful, dirty creatures he made. He came as a helpless baby to save you. He grew and experienced life in every way just like you. He experienced temptation just like you. He went through hormones just like you. He had to deal with people just like you. Still, he never sinned. The Creator of the cosmos confined himself to Palestine. The king of the world subjected himself to Roman rule. The Inventor of life and breath and everything good bled his life out in the excruciating form of torture on a cross made of wood. All because of your sin. *(If this has not made you lament your sin, you may need to dwell on it a little longer.)*

Sometimes our suffering is a direct result of our sin, as we see through David's heartbreaking loss of the child he and Bathsheba sinfully conceived.[6] Yet we are far better off facing those consequences with godly sorrow that leads to life and salvation than worldly grief (or lack thereof) that leads to regret, hopelessness, and ultimately despair.

Without godly sorrow over sin, the people Jesus suffered and died for will miss true repentance. Jesus didn't die to crush us. He died to crush our sin. He didn't hang on the cross to make us feel bad about ourselves. He hung on the cross to make us alive in him. The greatest news of all time is that Jesus not only died for our sins, but he didn't stay dead. And without godly sorrow that leads to repentance, we can't walk in and fully experience that same resurrected life he has purchased for us. Grief over sin means clinging to the Jesus who is alive and ruling and reigning over the cosmos even now. As David confessed his sin and depended on God for his cleansing, he was able to fully experience the abundant, Promised Land life. So can we if we do the same.

In addition to confessing our sin, we should cry out to God, admitting we do not have the strength or power to continue on our own. Most of David's laments fall into this category. In many Psalms, he talks about being surrounded by enemies on every side. His life is in jeopardy. There

---

6. 2 Sam 12:14.

is no way of escape. He is as good as dead. The only thing he can do is cry out to God that he cannot win. He cannot do it on his own. He needs God's mercy to even be able to fight. This confession of weakness takes a whole lot of strength.

We've already seen through Scripture that God fights our battles for us and with us. But often times, we like to think that we can do it ourselves. We still live as if we don't need God. We act as if he is more of an accessory than an essential. We call on him for help only when there is an emergency, signaling to the skies that we need him or running to him for him to kiss our boo boos. The truth of the matter is, he is the most essential part of our lives whether we realize it or not. In him all things hold together[7]—the universe, the galaxies, the planets, our bodies, the atoms of hydrogen that combine with oxygen to produce water. How could we not think it true for our very lives?

Confession of weakness and dependency on God is really a confession of strength. It may seem like an oxymoron or contradiction, yet it's anything but. Consider the question, *"Can God create a rock that is too heavy for himself to lift?"* The problem with that question is that it is a false dilemma and is actually contradictory. It's like saying, "Can the unlimited limit itself?" By nature, unlimited means that it is not limited, and by no means does it mean that it is limited because it can't be limited *(you may have to read that sentence a few times)*. To say that the all-powerful one can't create something that is too big for him does not limit his power. It just continues to show that he is all-powerful.

All that to say this: if God is so powerful that he can't create a rock too heavy for himself to lift, he is strong enough to handle any and all of the weight on your shoulders. And it is silly and foolish for us to try to carry that weight ourselves. So when we express our vulnerability and weakness, crying out to God for help amidst our hardships, we are yoking up with the all-powerful. And there's nothing weak about that.

Directional

In addition to being confessional, lamenting properly must also be directional. Not horizontally directed, but vertically directed towards God.

It's easy for people to make known their hurts, needs, and troubles through a post on social media, when venting to their spouse, or while

---

7. Col 1:17.

sitting in the break room at work. We often cry out to someone else about how hard life is, how bad someone has been to us, or how desperate our situation is. But in that sense, we are just complaining. People often complain, but people rarely lament.

When I say that lamenting is directional and that the direction is toward God, it means that if lamenting changes direction, it also changes definition. If it is no longer directed toward God, it is no longer considered a lament. Then it becomes a complaint, also known as grumbling. There's a huge difference. Not just in direction, but also in function.

It is possible to voice your suffering in the correct direction toward God and it still be a complaint. That is what the Israelites did, and as we learned previously, that caused them to waste forty years wandering in the desert instead of enjoying the fruitful, abundant life of the Promised Land. They had the right direction, but not the right posture.

So how do we properly lament without complaining? By speaking up and getting low. Not in volume or tone, but in posture. When things don't go our way in life, it is not wrong to humbly voice our disappointments, questions, and sorrow to God and those around us. It's ok to let others know we are struggling. But we should talk to God about our situation first and foremost more than we talk to other people about it.

When you are carrying something too heavy to bear, first look towards the heavens to where your help comes from instead of outward towards those who will only add their complaints to yours. God can handle our questions. He can handle our disappointment. He knows what we are thinking already, so we might as well voice it to him. But we should do so in a humble, reverent way towards God, crying out just as Job did, "though he slay me, I will hope in him."[8]

Actional

Complaining voices our suffering without regards to action. Lamenting voices our suffering by begging for action. Complaining is resting in your suffering. Lamenting is calling for help out of your suffering. Laments are actional, on our behalf and God's, because we are crying out for God to help us in our suffering and despair. It is beseeching God to act on our behalf.

Imagine yourself in a pit. A deep, dark, damp pit. Nobody likes pits, especially dark ones. You are literally down in the dumps in the pit of

8. Job 13:15.

despair with no way out. It's far too deep, and there's nothing in the pit with which you could use to dig or climb your way out. You are helpless. So what can you do? You have two options. Either (1) Cry to yourself about the despair of your situation, or (2) Cry out in hopes that another will hear you and come to your rescue. In the first scenario, you die. In the second, it is your only chance at life.

You cannot live an abundant life while throwing a pity party. Complaining will only rob your life of joy and blessing, just like it did for the wandering Israelites. Now, God will never abandon you in your pity party because he is patient with us in our affliction, but when you can do nothing, crying out for another to act on your behalf is the only option that can bring you life. The truth is we can do nothing on our own, but God can do everything. Therefore, when we properly lament and cry out to him, we can and should expect God to act on our behalf. Remember a point from the last chapter: He is always working even when we can't see it. Take Phil 4:6–7 to heart: "Do not be anxious about anything, but in everything by prayer and supplication with thanksgiving let your requests be made known to God. And the peace of God, which surpasses all understanding, will guard your hearts and your minds in Christ Jesus."

Hopeful

Hope, the fourth major distinguishing mark of laments, is a powerful thing. Hope is what drives us to stay up late at night to catch the final seconds of overtime—"I *hope* my team wins!" It is what compels us to make plans at an outdoor venue during rainy season—"I *hope* it doesn't rain." It is what makes us dress up and smell good and act slightly out of character to woo that special someone—"I *hope* she likes me." Yet this is *"hope so"* hope. We hope all the time. But in these circumstances, we're never certain though. Maybe they'll lose. Maybe it'll rain. Maybe she won't like me. But hope in God is certain. Always.

Hope in God is certain because even if the outcome is not what you desired, you know his ways are higher than yours.[9] Even if you never see the good, you know he is working for your good.[10] Even if this world causes you pain, you know this world is not your home.[11] Even if you suffer the

---

9. Isa 55:8–9.
10. Rom 8:28.
11. Phil 3:20; Heb 11:8–9; 13:14.

rest of your life, you know this isn't the only life you'll live. He's making all things new.[12] So no matter how intense or long lasting your suffering may be, you can say that this light and momentary affliction is preparing for you an eternal weight of glory beyond all comparison.[13] You can grieve amidst your suffering and still be full of hope.

Without pain and suffering, we would never know what it means to hope. Fire requires wood. Wood that is broken, torn apart, dried out. Flowers spring from seeds. Seeds that are buried, broken, seemingly dead. Suffering does not mean we lack hope. It is the fuel for hope. There is no need for hope apart from being the underdog, the hurting, the cast aside, the wronged, the scared, the weak. Many people are content with staying in their suffering. But hope is what propels us forward. Hope is what takes us from our desperation to our destination. Hope is what we are given when we make our requests known to God, expecting him to hear and expecting him to answer. It is what allows us to live beyond our suffering while amidst our suffering.

Because laments are directed toward God, and because God is the only one who can do something about our helpless state, we always have a reason to hope. Laments are a wonderful tool to be able to process our struggles and share the hope that we have for life beyond what the world can offer. As Mark Vroegop states in his book *Dark Clouds, Deep Mercy*:

> In lament, we are honest with the struggles of life while also reminding ourselves that God never stops being God. His steadfast love never ends. He is sufficient. Therefore, our hope is not in a change of circumstances but in the promise of a God who never stops being merciful—even when dark clouds loom.[14]

Dear sufferer, what are you hoping in? If it's in anything but Jesus Christ, you will always be disappointed. But you don't have to wallow in your despair. There is a God who hears your cries. You don't have to face your hardships alone. There is a God who is with you and for you. You don't have to live life in a constant state of disappointment. There is a God who loves you and promises that one day the struggle will end. And until that day, you can still experience abundance of life, because in Christ and through Christ, there is always hope. Let that fuel your walking and breathing and talking and thinking and crying and singing. And may you and I

---

12. Rev 21:1–5.
13. 2 Cor 4:17.
14. Vroegop, *Dark Clouds, Deep Mercy*, 113–14.

be able to confidently sing the chorus of Peterson's song I referenced at the beginning of this chapter:

> 'Cause You never let go, You never let go,
> You led me by the hand into a land of green and gold
> And You never let go, You never let go
> Your love endures forever, wherever I go
> After all these years
> That's all that I know

Chapter Six

Giving Thanks in All Circumstances
The Battle of Gratitude

Psalm 136:23–26

²³ It is he who remembered us in our low estate,
  for his steadfast love endures forever;
²⁴ and rescued us from our foes,
  for his steadfast love endures forever;
²⁵ he who gives food to all flesh,
  for his steadfast love endures forever.

²⁶ Give thanks to the God of heaven,
  for his steadfast love endures forever.

THERE'S NO DENYING THAT our culture idolizes materialism. The physical. The seen. The tangible. "What you see is what you get" is the driving mantra for many people who have no faith in something more than this life. When you live with this worldview, it's easy to buy into the belief, "You Only Live Once, so might as well live it up!" YOLO has a nice ring to it, but it's not all glamorous. In fact, it's bad news for billions of people if they only live once, and their life is *this bad*! That is the epitome of hopelessness—being stuck in suffering with no certainty of a way out. But fortunately, YOLO isn't reality because this life is not all there is. The truth is you were made for more. An eternity more.

Many materialistic scientists scoff at Christians for their presuppositions about God, all the while blind to the fact that if God truly does exist, they would never know it because they assume that the immaterial (that which cannot be seen/evaluated) isn't real. For those of us who walk by faith, that belief seems foolish, but it's been sold to the majority of our world. Look at this quote about suffering from Richard Dawkins, a renowned atheistic evolutionary biologist, who has no belief in anything outside our material world:

> The total amount of suffering per year in the natural world is beyond all decent contemplation. During the minute that it takes me to compose this sentence, thousands of animals are being eaten alive, many others are running for their lives, whimpering with fear, others are slowly being devoured from within by rasping parasites, thousands of all kinds are dying of starvation, thirst, and disease. . .In a universe of electrons and selfish genes, blind physical forces and genetic replication, some people are going to get hurt, other people are going to get lucky, and you won't find any rhyme or reason in it, nor any justice. The universe that we observe has precisely the properties we should expect if there is, at bottom, no design, no purpose, no evil, no good, nothing but pitiless indifference.[1]

No wonder so many are without hope! People who believe these lies have the short game in mind thinking it's the long game. They have no concept of a real eternity without suffering. But we as Christ's followers do because we know and believe in what is promised—a world with no more death or mourning or crying or pain, for the old order of things will pass away.[2] That is what Christians get a glimpse of now, even amidst our suffering. That is why the abundant life is still possible even though we live in a broken and depraved world. Because of the eternity purchased, provided, and prepared by God, there is hope. For any and every circumstance you face. And for that, we always have reason to give thanks.

---

1. Dawkins, *River Out of Eden*, 131–32.
2. Rev 21: 4.

David lived with this kind of hope in heaven even though he suffered much while on earth. When he received news that his infant son was near death, which God told him would be the consequence to his sin with Bathsheba and the murder of her husband, David fasted and prayed. He beseeched the throne of God. He begged for his son's life to be spared. He laid on his floor, covered in sackcloth and ashes. He wouldn't eat. He wouldn't drink. He was desperate, hoping that maybe God would change his mind and spare his son.

I've experienced similar desperation in the ICU hallway as I watched doctors rush into my sister's room to try to keep her alive. They were able to bring her back, and we had a sliver of hope that she would make it after that. But then her body would fail again, and this pattern kept happening three or four more times. We prayed and prayed and prayed, crying out to God, *"Please, spare her life!"* David prayed and prayed and prayed, too. He had seen God move on his behalf in miraculous ways before, and he begged God to do so again. But David's son died. Even amidst his prayers. So did my sister, Jaimie.

How to Move Forward in the Face of Suffering

When people face the darkness and pain of searing loss, most never move beyond it. At least those without eternal hope seem not to. But David's response to the death of his seven-day-old son is countercultural and counterintuitive. When he found out that his son had died, he immediately stopped fasting and praying. He got up and showered, put on some nice clothes, and went to church. He didn't go to yell at God or wallow in self-pity. He went to worship.

God's decision to take his son had been made, and there was nothing David could do to change it. David's heart was undoubtedly broken, but he still chose to honor God in that moment. And after he worshipped, he ate. Maybe it was a juicy burger with fries and a milkshake, who knows. But if you've ever experienced the searing pain of losing someone you love, you likely did not feel like eating afterwards. There's a pit in your stomach that no food can satisfy, and David probably felt it, too. Everyone expected him to continue fasting and wailing just as he was doing before, but he didn't. He stopped, worshipped, and ate. David continued living. How? Because he trusted God, and he knew he would see his son again. See the exchange between him and his servants in 2 Sam 12:21–23:

²¹ Then his servants said to him, "What is this thing that you have done? You fasted and wept for the child while he was alive; but when the child died, you arose and ate food." ²² He said, "While the child was still alive, I fasted and wept, for I said, 'Who knows whether the Lord will be gracious to me, that the child may live?' ²³ But now he is dead. Why should I fast? Can I bring him back again? I shall go to him, but he will not return to me."

Yes, David was still sad. Of course his grief did not end in that moment. He would forever be changed by the overwhelming sorrow of his loss and deal with it for the rest of his life. But not as one without hope. David knew he would see his son again. When he said, "I shall go to him, but he will not return to me," I don't believe that David was simply saying, "I hope I die, too, because he can't come back to life." His actions give evidence otherwise because he continued living. David had hope in life beyond the grave, even though it would be years before he would be reunited with his son.

If you have no hope in heaven, despair will swallow up every ounce of hope you thought you once had whenever you face the death of a loved one or when facing the prospect of death yourself. But Christians can continue living in the face of death, just like David did. And whatever circumstance you may be facing, dear reader, God wants you to keep on living, too.

Hope has been such a driving factor in my ability to continue living amidst suffering that when my wife and I found out we were expecting a baby girl four years after my sister's death, we decided to use a combination of the name Jaimie and Hope. Our daughter's namesake is a glimmer of hope from heaven, and she is a constant reminder of God's goodness and sustaining grace through our suffering. Her name has double meaning for my wife, who was burdened by not being able to conceive after months of fervently praying for a second child. Hope-deferred made her heart sick,[3] especially when several friends of hers announced their pregnancies during our struggle. But the year-long period of waiting for the blessing of another child was producing in us perseverance; and perseverance, character; and character, hope.[4] And that hope did not disappoint. Not because we finally received what we had been praying for, but because hope—in Jesus, in eternal life, in God's goodness despite our pain—was the one constant we could

---

3. Prov 13:12.
4. Rom 5:3–5.

cling to. It kept us going. It kept us trusting. It kept us waiting on God to fulfill his promises to us. Promises for an abundant life.

The Cost of Complaining

Not every promise fulfilled seems abundant or good by the world's standards. Take the Israelites for example. They had seen God split the Red Sea and provide manna from heaven, and still they grumbled and complained. The desert was probably hot. The views were probably monotonous. Their tents were probably not their dream homes. Even though God had provided for them, it wasn't exactly in ways they wanted or thought they deserved. And their ingratitude turned into bitterness. Therefore, the trek to the Promised Land that should have taken weeks took years, and many never lived to see the promise fulfilled.

Just like the Israelites, when we forget God's blessings and complain, we miss out on the abundant life God has for us. But the good news is, there's a cure for grumbling! It's being grateful to God for what you have. Gratitude is the cure to many ills. You can't be bitter against someone you are grateful for. You can't be discontent with something that you are thankful for. If you choose gratitude amidst your suffering, you are not basing your response on your present circumstances. You are choosing to act upon a reality that you do not yet see. Just because you don't yet see it doesn't mean it is any less real. Just because it hasn't been actualized doesn't mean it is not actual. Gratitude and hope go hand in hand.

Choosing gratitude amidst suffering puts our real-life hope into action. For the non-Christian, this world is the closest thing to heaven they will ever experience. And I don't know about you, but it seems to me that this world is getting worse with each passing day. Thank goodness the abundant life is so much more than what can be seen! God isn't limited to blessing us in only tangible or expected ways. His ways are higher than our ways, and his ways—though maybe different than ours—are always good. Therefore, we always have a reason to give thanks no matter what we face in this life.

Remember when we talked about God's will for your life in chapter 2? 1 Thessalonians 5:18 says, "give thanks in all circumstances; for this is the will of God in Christ Jesus for you." Whatever the circumstance may be that you find yourself in, you are commanded to give thanks.

PART TWO—DAVID

Gratitude is a battle. A daily battle. A moment-by-moment battle. It's easy to be thankful when times are good and we have all we want. But it's a battle when our situation is dire.

It's interesting that the apostle Paul (inspired by the Holy Spirit) is the one who wrote the command to give thanks in all circumstances. He suffered more than just about anyone in the New Testament. Suffering was literally part of his calling by God.[5] Here are some of his hardships he recounts in 2 Cor 11:24–29:

> [24] Five times I received at the hands of the Jews the forty lashes less one. [25] Three times I was beaten with rods. Once I was stoned. Three times I was shipwrecked; a night and a day I was adrift at sea; [26] on frequent journeys, in danger from rivers, danger from robbers, danger from my own people, danger from Gentiles, danger in the city, danger in the wilderness, danger at sea, danger from false brothers; [27] in toil and hardship, through many a sleepless night, in hunger and thirst, often without food, in cold and exposure. [28] And, apart from other things, there is the daily pressure on me of my anxiety for all the churches. [29] Who is weak, and I am not weak? Who is made to fall, and I am not indignant?

Though the apostle Paul went through all this and more, he commands those in Thessalonica to give thanks no matter what they were facing. His words still apply to us today. When a loved one dies, give thanks to God for the life they lived. When your child is wayward, give thanks to God that he loves them more than you ever could. When you lose your job, give thanks to God for all the ways he has provided for you before. There is always reason to give thanks.

Giving Thanks Consistently

Long before the apostle Paul, King David understood the need to give thanks, even in difficult circumstances. In the Psalms, "give thanks" is found thirty-seven times. I think Paul and David knew something we tend to forget. Constant and consistent gratitude is a necessary component of the abundant life.

In Psalm 136, likely written by David, he starts off saying:

> [1] Give thanks to the Lord, for he is good,
> for his steadfast love endures forever.

---

5. Acts 9:16.

> ² Give thanks to the God of gods,
>   for his steadfast love endures forever.
> ³ Give thanks to the Lord of lords,
>   for his steadfast love endures forever.

He then recounts many of the ways God had come through for his people in the past, including delivering them from Egypt, parting the Red Sea, leading his people through the wilderness, striking down kings and nations to give them the Promised Land, and remembering, rescuing, and providing their every need. After each statement of how God has come through for his people, we see this phrase repeated: "for his steadfast love endures forever."

God not only provides in countless ways for you. He loves you. And his love for you never stops. It is steadfast. It endures forever. David experienced this through the history of God's provision in leading his people to the Promised Land. Even amidst some bleak years of following the ways of the world, David realized that God never left his people and always provided. That is cause to give thanks! It was all because of God's steadfast love. And it is interesting to note that David had been taught all these great and mighty deeds God had done for his people. Just like the twelve memorial stones were set up some four hundred years prior to remind God's people of his deliverance, David remembered and gave thanks.

After recounting all the myriad ways that God had provided for his people, because of his steadfast love, David concludes by saying, "Give thanks to the God of heaven, for his steadfast love endures forever." He begins and ends by commanding the people to give thanks to God. And the people in David's time and beyond sang this psalm as a thankful reminder of God's goodness. Read what Charles Spurgeon says about Psalm 136:

> It was sung in Solomon's temple (2 Ch 7:3,6), and by the armies of Jehoshaphat when they sang themselves into victory in the wilderness of Tekoa. From the striking form of it we should infer that it was a popular hymn among the Lord's ancient people. Most hymns with a solid, simple chorus become favourites with congregations, and this is sure to have been one of the best beloved. It contains nothing but praise. It is tuned to rapture, and can only be fully enjoyed by a devoutly grateful heart.⁶

Like David and the armies marching into battle, you can and should sing the song of gratitude and victory as well. Gratitude breeds gratitude.

6. Spurgeon, "Psalm 136."

When you take time to thank God, you realize how much you have to be thankful for. When you pause to look back on God's faithfulness in your life, you realize how overwhelmingly much he has done. He has given you life, salvation, family, friends, material needs, even some wants. But even when God takes away, may we be able to give thanks and say along with Job, "blessed be the name of the Lord,"[7] because God has always been gracious. He has always been good. He has always been faithful. And when you start thanking God for all the blessings he has given you, you then start to realize you really have been given an abundant life in him.

Dear reader, is your heart devoutly grateful? Can you still worship though you hurt? Can you still eat though the pit in your stomach is deep? Can you still live though you have experienced death? Yes. Because death is not the end of the story. Life is. And with God, there is abundance of life.

---

7. Job 1:21

Chapter Seven

Pairing Laments with Praise
The Battle of Worship

Psalm 34:1-7

¹ I will bless the Lord at all times;
his praise shall continually be in my mouth.
² My soul makes its boast in the Lord;
let the humble hear and be glad.
³ Oh, magnify the Lord with me,
and let us exalt his name together!

⁴ I sought the Lord, and he answered me
and delivered me from all my fears.
⁵ Those who look to him are radiant,
and their faces shall never be ashamed.
⁶ This poor man cried, and the Lord heard him
and saved him out of all his troubles.
⁷ The angel of the Lord encamps
around those who fear him, and delivers them.

PART TWO—DAVID

THROUGHOUT MY YEARS OF working closely with grieving Christians, one common thread I have heard from many people about what has helped them amidst their grief is music. Specifically *worship* music. Why do you think that is? Because worship rightly frames both our mind and our heart. Even and especially amidst suffering, we should praise God.

One of the most powerful and meaningful moments I have experienced in a church service was shortly after my sister passed. I was standing in the front row. The world around me had disappeared. And against all my body and mind was wanting to do, I lifted my hands in worship, in complete surrender to God. Another instance I vividly remember during a different church service is seeing a man who had just lost his father lift his hands in worship with tears streaming down his face. Maybe you have experienced something similar at a time in your life when you were hurting but still chose to worship God in reverent surrender. If not, maybe you should try. Look up the song "Though You Slay Me" by Shane and Shane, close your eyes, and worship as Job did amidst his suffering when he said, "Though he slay me, I will hope in him."[1] God is worthy of our worship whether we think he is or not. And God is worthy of our worship whether we feel like worshiping him or not.

Charles Spurgeon modeled this well. Though he was one of the greatest preachers of all time, he battled daily mental, emotional, and physical distress. He was open about his hardship, referring to his bouts of depression as "fainting fits." He often called himself a "prisoner" and wept without knowing why.[2] Hear how one person describes his sufferings:[3]

> Aged twenty-two, as pastor of a large church and with twin babies at home to look after, he was preaching to thousands in the Surrey Gardens Music Hall when pranksters yelled "fire," starting a panic to exit the building which killed seven and left twenty-eight severely injured. His mind was never the same again. His wife, Susannah, wrote, "My beloved's anguish was so deep and violent, that reason seemed to totter in her throne, and we sometimes feared that he would never preach again."[4]
>
> Then, from the age of thirty-three, physical pain became a large and constant feature of life for him. He suffered from a burning kidney

1. Job 13:15.
2. "11 Reasons Spurgeon Was Depressed."
3. Reeves, "Did You Know."
4. Ray, "Life of Susannah Spurgeon," 166.

PAIRING LAMENTS WITH PRAISE

inflammation called Bright's Disease, as well as gout, rheumatism, and neuritis. The pain was such that it soon kept him from preaching for one-third of the time. Added to that, overwork, stress, and guilt about the stress began to take their toll. And all this was in the public eye and was jumped on by his many critics, not making it easier to bear. The suffering, they argued rather predictably, was a judgment from God.

The pain, the politics, the opposition, and the overwork (as well as bereavements, like that of his young grandson) all affected him deeply, if in waves. So much so that today he would almost certainly be diagnosed as clinically depressed and treated with medication and therapy. The depression could hit him so intensely that, he once said, "I could say with Job, 'My soul chooseth strangling rather than life' [Job 7:15]. I could readily enough have laid violent hands upon myself, to escape from my misery of spirit."[5]

Amidst his many sufferings, Spurgeon found solace in the Psalms, and he produced one of the greatest works on the Psalms titled, *The Treasury of David*. He preached over four hundred sermons throughout his ministry from this work and invested twenty years to produce the seven-volume commentary. The first volume was published at the age of thirty-one and the last one published seven years before his death at the age of fifty-five. It is his "magnum opus" and is even more impressive and meaningful knowing that he wrote much of it while suffering so severely.[6] Perhaps he wrote so prolifically on the Psalms not necessarily *while* he suffered, but *because* he suffered.

The Psalms are a balm to the weary soul. They are the church's original hymn book. In them, our gaze is lifted heavenward, where our gaze should be fixed in worship. They teach us how to not only lament but how and why we can worship amidst our pain. Vroegop says it beautifully:

> You might think lament is the opposite of praise. It isn't. Instead, lament is a path to praise as we are led through our brokenness and disappointment. The space between brokenness and God's mercy is where this song is sung. Think of lament as the transition between pain and promise.[7]

This path of pairing worship with lament helps us remember God is still on his throne even when our life seems like it is falling apart. God is

---

5. Spurgeon, *Metropolitan Tabernacle Pulpit Sermons*, 200.
6. McKinley, "Significance of the Psalms for Spurgeon."
7. Vroegop, *Dark Clouds, Deep Mercy*, 28.

worthy of our worship, always, even amidst our suffering. Let's take a look at a few specific Psalms and see some of David's praises and laments while he was fighting battles in the Promised Land, and in each excerpt, I'll include some of Spurgeon's take on it. I encourage you to read the psalm from your Bible first and then read the excerpt. I pray it will lead you to worship amidst your battle, too.

Psalm 3

While David was fleeing from his son Absalom, fearing for his life, he saw reason to praise God amidst lamenting the situation he was in. Though people said that God was not rescuing him, David knew the truth, and cried, "But you, O Lord, are a shield about me, my glory, and the lifter of my head" (vs 3). After he finally took time to rest, knowing he could be killed in his sleep, he said, "I woke again, for the Lord sustained me" (vs 5). When he cried out again to be rescued, he concluded with, "Salvation belongs to the Lord; your blessing be on your people!" (vs 8).

Even in the face of a wayward child, the fear of death, and his own son seeking to kill him, David found reason to worship God. Whatever situation you are in, amidst your crying out to God, there is yet reason to praise him. Hear the heart of Spurgeon in reference to the final verse of this psalm, about God's salvation and blessing to his people:

> "Thy blessing is upon thy people." Divine, discriminating, distinguishing, eternal, infinite, immutable love, is a subject for constant adoration. Pause, my soul, at this *Selah*, and consider thine own interest in the salvation of God; and if by humble faith thou art enabled to see Jesus as thine by his own free gift of himself to thee, if this greatest of all blessings be upon thee, rise up and sing—
>
> "Rise, my soul! adore and wonder!
> Ask, 'O why such love to me?'
> Grace hath put me in the number
> Of the Saviour's family:
> Hallelujah!
> Thanks, eternal thanks, to thee!"[8]

---

8. Spurgeon, "Psalm 3."

Psalm 18

When David had been delivered by God from King Saul, the first words out of his mouth were, "I love you, O Lord, my strength" (vs 1). He describes God as the one, "who is worthy to be praised" (vs 3). David then paints a picture of the grandeur of God, a God worthy of worship. A God who hears David's lament "from his temple" (vs 6), and responds to him by "part[ing] the heavens and [coming] down" to trample the "dark clouds" engulfing him (vs 9). God is powerful. Thunder comes from his voice (vs 13). I don't know about you, but the imagery David paints of God "reach[ing] down from on high and [taking] hold of me," (vs 16) makes me feel safe. Like God is holding me in the palm of his hands. And if "he drew [David] out of deep waters," he can do the same for us. David then speaks of God's character as merciful, blameless, and pure (vs 25–26).

Rather than boasting in how he has been delivered, David boasted in the God who delivers. He says, "This God—his way is perfect; the word of the Lord proves true; he is a shield for all those who take refuge in him" (vs 30). After many other words of praise, David concludes with, "For this I will praise you, O Lord, among the nations, and sing to your name" (vs 49).

Whether amidst the battle or after the victory, you can sing the same, because God is worthy, and he is working. Whether he has pulled you out of the pit or not, he is able and he is to be praised. In Spurgeon's exposition of this psalm, he shares these encouraging words: "The Psalm concludes in the same loving spirit which shone upon its commencement; happy are they who can sing on from love to love, even as the pilgrims marched from strength to strength."[9]

Dear reader, you can sing as well, because you are greatly loved, and God is strengthening you through whatever trial you may be facing.

Psalm 30

When we cry out to God in lament, it causes us to cry out to him in another way—praise—as evidenced by David in this psalm. Multiple times David speaks of crying out or calling to God and beseeching God to hear him (vss 2, 8, 10). This psalm concludes with his wailing being turned into dancing, and the despair of his lament turned to the joy of praise (vs 11). A lifetime

---

9. Spurgeon, "Psalm 18."

of giving thanks is the outcome of crying out to God and trusting him for deliverance (vs 12).

The substance of David's cries that eventually lead to praise can be seen at the beginning of this psalm by two parallel verbs: extol and draw. The first words he utters is that he will "extol" or "exalt" the Lord, and the reason is directly given: because God had "drawn him up" or "lifted" him out of the depths (vs 1). "Extol" implies motion up and away from yourself, as if someone were pushing a small child up to safety onto a high rock in rising waters. On the other hand, to "draw" someone up means to lift them up from below and towards yourself, as if drawing water from a well. It can also be used to describe the act of pulling someone out of danger, such as pulling a person out of raging waters with a rope to save them from drowning.[10] David had experienced this deliverance in his own life. God had pulled him up, which in turn, led David to lift the Lord *high*. Likewise, God has done the same for us, which should lead us to a similar response. Hear Spurgeon's heart regarding our rightful response of praise to God from these verses:

> It would be a shameful crime, if, after receiving God's mercies, we should forget to praise him. God would not have our tongues lie idle while so many themes for gratitude are spread on every hand. He would have no [mute] children in the house. They are all to sing in heaven, and therefore they should all sing on earth.[11]

Think back on the times you have cried to God. Can you see the deliverance he has given? Let that lead you to "extol" and lift high the Lord.

Psalm 34

Like Psalm 30, Psalm 34 is another recounting of David's many cries to the Lord which led him to praise. He says God's "praise shall continually be in my mouth" (vs 1). Not only do we see, again, that laments lead to praise, but this psalm is also a treasure trove of comfort for the hurting, fearful, and brokenhearted. Many of the passages are worth hiding in our heart for the exact moments we need them (vss 4, 8, 10, 15, 18). A common refrain, mentioned repeatedly, is that God hears the cries of the righteous, and he delivers them from trouble (vss 7, 9, 15, 17, 19, 22). David is remembering,

---

10. Wilson, *Psalms Volume 1*, 515.
11. Spurgeon, "Psalm 30."

in this psalm, a specific instance of his life where he was fearful yet trusted God. You can read the full context of what he is referring to in 1 Sam 21:10–15, when David acts like he is crazy while in the court of the Philistines so they would let him go.[12] And the plan worked. God delivered David.

Now I'm not telling you to act crazy in order to gain God's deliverance in a sticky situation. But I am saying that following after God is a prerequisite for deliverance by God.

Think back on a time of your life where you were fearful, hurt, or brokenhearted. How did God provide for you? If you feared the Lord and followed after him, I'm certain he has provided for you in the past and will provide for you even now. The application of this psalm can be summarized with four imperatives for us to live out.[13] First, bless the Lord (vss 1–3). Second, seek the Lord (vss 4–8). Third, fear the Lord (vss 9–16). Fourth, trust the Lord (vss 17–22). This psalm reminds us that no matter what we may be going through, we can trust in God's faithfulness and goodness. He is a God who is close to us in our pain and who saves those who trust in him when they are in need. So you will always have reason to praise. As Spurgeon eloquently says of these verses, "He who praises God for mercies shall never want a mercy for which to praise. To bless the Lord is never unreasonable."[14]

Psalm 57

This psalm gives us a glimpse into David trusting in God while being a fugitive for a day. David had fled from King Saul, who was trying to kill him, found protection in the cave of Adullam (1 Sam 22:1), and later moved to a cave in Engedi (1 Sam 24:1–3). Sleep is one of the hardest things to do when worried and fearful, and it is one of the most visible expressions of trusting in God amidst hardship. In this cave, as a fugitive, David lies down (vs 4) and he awakes (vs 8) later. Amidst turmoil, "God quieted his heart and gave him the sleep he needed."[15]

Warren Weirsbe captures the sentiment of David here well, and perhaps you can find strength from his words: "Better to be in the will of God

---

12. Wilson, *Psalms Volume 1*, 567.
13. Wiersbe, *Wiersbe Bible Commentary: Old Testament*, 915–16.
14. Spurgeon, "Psalm 34."
15. Wiersbe, *Wiersbe Bible Commentary: Old Testament*, 939.

in a cave than out of His will in a king's palace."¹⁶ This psalm shows us what this book has continually been stating, that God doesn't always remove us from our troubles, but he is with us "in the midst of" them (vs 4). He "provides an enduring confidence even in the face of all evidence to the contrary."¹⁷ This should lead our hearts and mouths to lift high the repeated refrain of David, "Be exalted, O God" (vss 5, 11).

You have reason to praise even amidst your suffering because God is fulfilling his purposes for you (vs 2). Like David, you can fix your heart on God and rest in his sovereignty and goodness. Hear Spurgeon's plea in his take on verse 7:

> O God, my heart is fixed. I am resolved to trust thee, to serve thee, and to praise thee. Twice does he declare this to the glory of God who thus comforts the souls of his servants. Reader, it is surely well with thee, if thy once roving heart is now firmly fixed upon God and the proclamation of his glory. I will sing and give praise. Vocally and instrumentally will I celebrate thy worship. With lip and with heart will I ascribe honour to thee. Satan shall not stop me, nor Saul, nor the Philistines, I will make Adullam ring with music, and all the caverns thereof echo with joyous song. Believer, make a firm decree that your soul in all seasons shall magnify the Lord.
>
> "Sing, though sense and carnal reason
> Fain would stop the joyful song:
> Sing, and count it highest treason
> For a saint to hold his tongue."¹⁸

Psalm 59

Psalm 59 is a psalm of trust in God in the midst of enemies and danger. These dangers are like wild dogs who snarl, bare their fangs, nip at our heals, and threaten to undo us.¹⁹ In this psalm, David cries out to God for deliverance from these enemies who rise up against him. He asks God to arise and defend him, to vindicate him and rescue him from these snarling dogs. Despite the threat of his enemies, David declares his trust in God,

16. Wiersbe, *The Wiersbe Bible Commentary: Old Testament*, 939.
17. Wilson, *Psalms Volume 1*, 831.
18. Spurgeon, "Psalm 57."
19. Wilson, *Psalms Volume 1*, 855.

stating that he will sing of the Lord's strength and protection (vss 16–17). David's example encourages us to sing and make music to the Lord as a sign of our trust and praise. When we praise God and give thanks for his protection and care, it strengthens our faith and reminds us of his faithfulness.

Though these dog-like evildoers were surrounding David, they were of no threat to God. And though hardships may surround you now, God is not worried. When David was fearful because of his circumstances, God laughed (vs 8). Not at David but at David's enemies. They thought they held power, but they were nothing under the mighty hand of God. It is the same with you. God is triumphant over all his enemies, and if you are not walking as an enemy of God, your enemies are God's enemies as well. And God is always victorious over his enemies.

Read the words of Spurgeon on this psalm as he dwells on where our strength comes from and what our boasting should be in:

> Strength has been overcome by strength; not by the hero's own prowess, but by the might of God alone. See how the singer girds himself with the almightiness of God, and calls it all his own by faith. Sweet is the music of experience, but it is all for God; there is not even a stray note for man, for self, or for human helpers. For God is my defense, and the God of my mercy. With full assurance he claims possession of the Infinite as his protection and security. He sees God in all, and all his own. Mercy rises before him, undisturbed and manifold, for he feels he is undeserving, and security is with him, undisturbed and impregnable, for he knows that he is safe in divine keeping.[20]

Psalm 63

This is a psalm of trust in God in times of drought and dryness. David spent much time in the wilderness in his early years when he was fleeing from Saul. He knew what it was to be thirsty, not just physically, but also spiritually. In this psalm, David longs for God and seeks him with all his heart, declaring that he will praise and honor him as long as he lives (vss 1, 4). He describes God as the one who satisfies, and he states that he will trust in him and joyfully praise him (vss 5, 7). No matter how dry or difficult our circumstances may be, we can trust God to satisfy and sustain us.

---

20. Spurgeon, "Psalm 59."

David also describes his desire to be in God's presence, stating that he will seek him in the morning and meditate on him throughout the day (vss 1, 6–7). He declares that he will remember God's faithfulness and love, even in times of drought and dryness (vs 3). Even with parched lips you can still praise God. When we do so, it helps to strengthen our faith and bring us closer to God, which is where our strength and sustenance is found. As David did, so let us turn to God in times of drought and trust in his faithfulness and love to sustain us. "Because your steadfast love is better than life, my lips will praise you" (vs 3). Spurgeon sums up the sentiment of this psalm well:

> A weary place and a weary heart make the presence of God the more desirable: if there be nothing below and nothing within to cheer, it is a thousand mercies that we may look up and find all we need. How frequently have believers traversed in their experience this *dry and thirsty land,* where spiritual joys are things forgotten! and how truly can they testify that the only true necessity of that country is the near presence of their God! The absence of outward comforts can be borne with serenity when we walk with God; and the most lavish multiplication of them avails not when he withdraws. Only after God, therefore, let us pant. Let all desires be gathered into one. Seeking first the kingdom of God—all else shall be added unto us.[21]

Though the explanations of these psalms were brief, my prayer is that you would (1) learn to search the psalms yourself for sustenance and strength along the journey, and (2) see the need for praise to be interspersed with lament. It is a battle in itself to praise God when your heart is downcast. But if you are truly lamenting, you know God hears your cry. And for God to hear your cry is for him to act. In the Old Testament, God's hearing and acting are one in the same. That's not only true of the psalms of David, but it's true of you. You have reason to worship God because he is always working. Even when you can't see it.

---

21. Spurgeon, "Psalm 63."

Chapter Eight

Connecting Through Real-Life Laments
The Battle of Honest Expression

Lamentations 3:19–24

[19]"Remember my affliction and my wanderings,
the wormwood and the gall!
[20]My soul continually remembers it
and is bowed down within me.

[21]But this I call to mind,
and therefore I have hope:

[22]The steadfast love of the Lord never ceases;
his mercies never come to an end;
[23]they are new every morning;
great is your faithfulness.
[24]"The Lord is my portion," says my soul,
"therefore I will hope in him."

PART TWO—DAVID

YOU HAVE SEEN THE need to lament in the previous three chapters. Now it is time to hear from others' hearts in hopes that we would learn to let laments flow from our own. Within this chapter, you will find real-life laments from real people facing real struggles. There is a mixture of poetry, songs, and prayers coupled with some of the stories behind them. Some of these laments are from famous theologians or songwriters while others are from ordinary people who have learned what it means to cry out to God with hope amidst their suffering. These are powerful examples that will inspire you to put into practice what God is doing in your heart. As you read these heart-wrenching, yet hopeful pleas, may you be informed, encouraged, and inspired to cast your soul before the One who is big enough and gentle enough to handle it all.

My favorite Christmas song is "I Heard the Bells on Christmas Day." I know it is not a common one to be at the top of the list for most people, but it is my favorite because I find so much hope in it. It comes from the heart of a "57-year-old widowed father of six children, the oldest of which had been nearly paralyzed as his country fought a war against itself."[1] Henry Wadsworth Longfellow wrote the poem "Christmas Bells" on December 25, 1863, four years after his wife died in a tragic accident involving her dress catching fire. Longfellow had woken from a nap and sought to extinguish the flames at first with a rug and then with his own body. Despite his best efforts to save her, she died the next day, and he was so severely burned from the incident that he couldn't attend her funeral. He suffered such severe grief that he feared he would be sent to an asylum at times.

> The first Christmas after Fanny's death, Longfellow wrote, "How inexpressibly sad are all holidays." A year after the incident he wrote, "I can make no record of these days. Better leave them wrapped in silence. Perhaps someday God will give me peace." Longfellow's journal entry for December 1862 reads, "'A merry Christmas' say the children, but that is no more for me."[2]

Two years later his oldest son went off to fight in the Civil War. He was badly wounded and nearly paralyzed. Amidst these tragedies, on Christmas

---

1. Most of the details from the backstory and writing of "Christmas Bells" are taken from an article written by Justin Taylor for *The Gospel Coalition*. Taylor, "True Story of Pain and Hope."

2. Meyer, "I Heard the Bells."

Day 1863, Longfellow heard the church bells ringing and the singing of "peace on earth," which seemingly mocked the lack of peace he felt. He then "wrote a poem seeking to capture the dynamic and dissonance in his own heart and the world he observes around him that Christmas Day." Yet even in his despair, he writes with hope, as you can clearly see in the last stanza.

Christmas Bells

by Henry Wadsworth Longfellow

I heard the bells on Christmas Day
Their old, familiar carols play,
  And wild and sweet
  The words repeat
Of peace on earth, good-will to men!

And thought how, as the day had come,
The belfries of all Christendom
  Had rolled along
  The unbroken song
Of peace on earth, good-will to men!

Till ringing, singing on its way,
The world revolved from night to day,
  A voice, a chime,
  A chant sublime
Of peace on earth, good-will to men!

Then from each black, accursed mouth
The cannon thundered in the South,
  And with the sound
  The carols drowned
Of peace on earth, good-will to men!

It was as if an earthquake rent
The hearth-stones of a continent,
  And made forlorn
  The households born
Of peace on earth, good-will to men!

And in despair I bowed my head;
"There is no peace on earth," I said;
  "For hate is strong,
  And mocks the song
Of peace on earth, good-will to men!"

PART TWO—DAVID

Then pealed the bells more loud and deep:
"God is not dead, nor doth He sleep;
 The Wrong shall fail,
 The Right prevail,
With peace on earth, good-will to men."

The well-known and beloved hymn, "It is Well" was written out of immense grief and loss, too. The family of Horatio Gates Spafford traveled to Europe, and he intended to meet them soon after. But their ship was in a terrible collision, and his four daughters died with his wife alone surviving. This tragedy came after they lost their son a few years earlier and their wealth burned up in the Chicago fire. Spafford wrote the hymn as he passed over the spot where the ship sank. Hear his heart from his own words:

> "On Thursday last we passed over the spot where she went down in mid-ocean, the water three miles deep. But I do not think of our dear ones there. They are safe, folded, the dear lambs, and there, before very long, shall we be too. In the meantime, thanks to God, we have an opportunity to serve and praise him for His love and mercy to us and ours. I will praise him while I have my being. May we each one arise, leave all, and follow Him."[3]

It is Well

by Horatio Gates Spafford

When peace like a river attendeth my way,
When sorrows like sea billows roll;
Whatever my lot Thou hast taught me to say,
"It is well, it is well with my soul!"

 It is well with my soul!
It is well, it is well with my soul!

Tho' Satan should buffet, tho' trials should come,
Let this blest assurance control,
That Christ hath regarded my helpless estate,
And hath shed his own blood for my soul.

3. "It Is Well with My Soul."

CONNECTING THROUGH REAL-LIFE LAMENTS

My sin - oh, the bliss of this glorious thought!
My sin - not in part but the whole,
Is nailed to His cross and I bear it no more;
Praise the Lord, praise the Lord, oh my soul.

And, Lord, haste the day when the faith shall be sight,
The clouds be rolled back as a scroll,
The trump shall resound, and the Lord shall descend
A song in the night, oh my soul!

(the following verse was added later)

For me, be it Christ, be it Christ hence to live,
If Jordan above me shall roll,
No pang shall be mine, for in death as in life
Thou shalt whisper Thy peace to my soul.

Charles Wesley, the great English minister and hymnwriter, penned many poems upon the occasion of the death of his firstborn son. When his son was a year old, both child and mother contracted smallpox. Though Charles' wife survived, their child did not. Of the poems below, one is while their child is sick, and the other is on the occasion of his death on January 7, 1754. You can hear both the grief and the hope mixed together as he seeks to trust God amidst his hardest of times.

Prayer for a Sick Child[4]

by Charles Wesley

God of love, incline thine ear,
Hear a cry of grief and fear,
Hear an anxious Parent's cry,
Help, before my Isaac die.

All my comfort in distress,
All my earthly happiness,
Spare him still, the precious Loan;
Is he not my only Son?

Whom I did from Thee obtain
Must I give him back again?

4. Baker, *Representative Verse of Charles Wesley*, 279.

Can I with the blessing part?
Lord, Thou know'st a Mother's heart:

All its passionate excess.
All its yearning tenderness,
Nature's soft infirmity,
Is it not a drop from Thee?

For Thy own compassion's sake,
Give me then my Darling back
Rais'd as from the dead, to praise,
Love, and serve Thee all his days.

Speak, and at Thy powerful word,
Lo, the witness to his Lord,
Monument of grace divine,
Isaac lives, for ever Thine!

On the Death of a Child[5]

Charles Wesley

Dead! dead! the Child I lov'd so well!
  Transported to the world above!
I need no more my heart conceal:
  I never dar'd indulge my love:
But may I not indulge my grief,
And seek in tears a sad relief?

Mine earthly happiness is fled,
  His mother's joy, his father's hope,
(O had I dy'd in *Isaac's* stead)
  He *should* have liv'd, my age's prop,
He should have clos'd his father's eyes,
And follow'd me to paradise.

But hath not heaven, who first bestow'd,
  A right to take His gifts away?
I bow me to the sovereign God,
  Who snatch'd him from the evil day!
Yet nature *will* repeat her moan,
And fondly cry, "My son, my son!"

Turn from him, turn, officious thought!

---

5. Baker, *Representative Verse of Charles Wesley*, 252.

Officious thought presents again
The thousand little acts he wrought,
   Which wound my heart with soothing pain:
His looks, his winning gestures rise,
His waving hands, and laughing eyes!

Those waving hands no more shall move,
   Those laughing eyes shall smile no more:
He cannot now engage our love,
   With sweet insinuating power
Our weak unguarded hearts insnare,
And rival his Creator there.

From us, as we from him, secure,
   Caught to his heavenly Father's breast,
He waits, till we the bliss insure,
   From all these stormy sorrows rest,
And see him with our Angel stand,
To waft, and welcome us to land.

Katy Bowser Hutson is a modern-day poet and a mother. She has heard the words that no person ever wants to hear, "You have cancer." As she crawled her way through breast cancer, she wrote and walked away with a collection of poems on the other side. Poems of real-life lament. Hear her desperation and her hope in the following poem from her compilation, *Now I Lay Me Down to Fight*.

I Wish, I Miss, I Thank You[6]

by Katy Bowser Hutson

Today, I wish I had enough energy to play with my little boy.
But, today you have ordained that my guts reject food
And I will trust that you have done this on purpose,
That it is for my good.

Today, I wish I could be in a pumpkin patch with my daughter
She is playing with her cousins, and that is a good, good gift
I will praise you for it from my bed.
Your gifts are good.

6. Hutson, *Now I Lay Me Down to Fight*.

I miss my hair today,
I'm grieving the takeover of my breasts
But I do not need them, or I would have them.
I was never promised to make it through this world without battle scars
But you have promised to carry me safely through, heart safely tucked away in your own
Where no cancer, no doubt, no decay can get at it to harm it.

You never promised me that I would get to finish all of my creative projects.
But you do let me make, and I apologize for when I have been lazy
I thank you that you have indeed let me create, for good.

I thank you for my family, who are caring for my children, our home—
My mom, who keeps washing my sheets and making my bed.
My dad, who is painting my kitchen and making it sweet and lovely.
My husband, holding it all together, falling apart with me.
I thank you for this bed.

John Woolman (1720–1772)[7] was a Quaker preacher in the American colonies. He was greatly opposed to slavery and made it his mission to abolish it. He was one of America's first abolitionists. He only wore clothes with no dye in them because he was told it was done through slave labor. He would not accept hospitality from slave owners. He wrote extensively against slavery. He lived his life to abolish it, and within twenty-five years of his death, the American Quakers voluntarily abandoned slaveholding. While traveling for ministry in England, John Woolman would eventually die of smallpox. In the early part of his illness, he requested a friend to write the following prayer he recited:

> O Lord, my God! The amazing horrors of darkness were gathered around me, and covered me all over, and I saw no way to go forth; I felt the depth and extent of the misery of my fellow-creatures separated from the Divine harmony, and it was heavier than I could bear, and I was crushed under it; lifted up my hand, I stretched out my arm but there was none to help me; I look round about, and was amazed. In the depths of misery, O Lord, I remembered

7. Davies, *Communion of Saints*.

that Thou art omnipotent; that I had called Thee Father; and I felt that I loved Thee, and I was made quiet in my will, and I waited for deliverance from Thee. Thou hadst pity upon me, when no man could help me; I saw that meekness under suffering was showed to us in the most affecting example of Thy Son, and Thou taughest me to follow Him and I said, "Thy will, O Father, be done!"

Mark Vroegop has become an expert on the topic of laments, stemming from his book *Dark Clouds, Deep Mercy: Discovering the Grace of Lament*. He is a pastor who has experienced the searing pain of having a full-term stillborn child. Out of his pain, he wrote this book to help others lament. Within the book, he says:

> Sometimes my last prayer of the day is a faith-filled, promise-claiming lament. I climb into bed exhausted because all day I've had to wrestle with my thinking. When sorrow and weariness try to take over the closing moments of my day, I pray some thing like this: "Lord, I'm weary and tired. I'm discouraged, and I don't know how I'm going to do this again tomorrow. But I believe your mercies are going to be new when I wake up. I believe that I will never run out of your steadfast love. I'm trusting that you have enough grace for me for what I face. I'm going to sleep because I'm hoping in you."[8]

A friend of mine has battled an addiction that cost him much more than he ever realized he would have to pay. He has sought help and had moments of overcoming, but his sin landed him in jail. As a Christian should, he faced his sin head on and humbly accepted the consequences. But for over a year he has been without his wife, his kids, and his church family, engulfed in a world of darkness he has never known before. Even though his sentence is not long-term, there seems to be no end in sight. From his prison cell, he wrote this lament:

---

8. Vroegop, *Dark Clouds, Deep Mercy*, 113.

PART TWO—DAVID

A Lament from Prison

(published anonymously)

Cold steel, concrete, razor wire—
My landscape is a grey island in the green.
A self-made castaway, I'm bound by
Dimensions of the daily, living death
Of separation from those that I love.
The white-hot horrors of hands grasping
Across undefinable distance;
My children cry, "Daddy, I can't reach you!"
Words that simmer like the stuff of nightmares.
O God, my God, do you even care?
How long, Father?
Will the sun ever rise again?

Surely, this time my enemies
Will break through the walls.
I hear them all around, taunting me,
Haunting me, saying my God will not save.
At this rate they'll win the day.
Will you just sit there, silent, and leave me all alone?
Is this justice or violence for the things that I've done?
I'm out of options; my arrows are spent.
Their drums beat a death-rhythm hard against the gate.
Chanting, ranting, they sing to their gods
While mine makes me wait.
Will help ever come?

I cry out, pleading, with each breath you give.
Must a song be beautiful or warm?
Can it be blood-soaked and pitiful, a melody torn?
Because I don't feel like singing.
I feel like bringing the whole world crashing
Down with me into the shallow madness
Of callous rage.
Will you hold me, God? It's so dark.

Tender are the memories of mornings past,
Smoothing over sorrows while joy sleeps
Through lingering doubt, until that shining hour
To wake at last.

CONNECTING THROUGH REAL-LIFE LAMENTS

Professor and theologian Nicholas Wolterstorff tragically lost his twenty-five-year-old son, Eric, in a climbing accident. In the days following Eric's death, Dr. Wolterstorff began lamenting. He did not intend to publish his various laments, prayers, and thoughts, but he ended up compiling them and having them published for you and me in a book titled *Lament for a Son*. Though his laments are specific, they can help give voice to ours. I have included some that may aid in your personal laments.

> We took him too much for granted. Perhaps we all take each other too much for granted. The routines of life distract us; our own pursuits make us oblivious; our anxieties and sorrows, unmindful. The beauties of the familiar go unremarked. We do not treasure each other enough.
>
> He was a gift to us for twenty-five years. When the gift was finally snatched away, I realized how great it was. Then I could not tell him. An outpouring of letters arrived, many expressing appreciation for Eric. They all made me weep again: each word of praise a stab of loss.
>
> How can I be thankful, in his gone-ness, for what he was? I find I am. But the pain of the *no more* outweighs the gratitude of the *once was*. Will it always be so?
>
> I didn't know how much I loved him until he was gone.
>
> Is love like that?[9]

> On the way back I thought about tears. Our culture says that men must be strong and that the strength of a man in sorrow is to be seen in his tearless face. Tears are for women. Tears are signs of weakness and women are permitted to be weak. Of course it's better if they too are strong.
>
> But why celebrate stoic tearlessness? Why insist on never outwarding the inward when that inward is bleeding? Does enduring while crying not require as much strength as never crying? Must we always mask our suffering? May we not sometimes allow people to see and enter it? I mean, may *men* not do this?
>
> And why is it so important to act strong? I have been graced with the strength to endure. But I have been assaulted, and in the assault wounded, grievously wounded. Am I to pretend otherwise? Wounds are ugly, I know. They repel. But must they always be swathed?
>
> I shall look at the world through tears. Perhaps I shall see things that dry-eyed I could not see.[10]

---

9. Wolterstorff, *Lament for a Son*, 13.
10. Wolterstorff, *Lament for a Son*, 26.

> With every fiber of my being I long to talk with Eric again. When I mentioned this to someone, she asked what I would say. I don't know. Maybe I would just blurt out something silly. That would be good enough for a beginning. We could take it from there. Every day I wonder, and some days I doubt, whether that talk will ever take place. But then comes that insistent voice: "Remember, I made all this and raised my own son from the dead, so I can also..."
>
> I know, I know. But why don't you raise mine now? Why did you ever let him die? If creation took just six days, why does re-creation take so agonizingly long? If your conquest of primeval chaos went so quickly, why must your conquest of sin and death and suffering be so achingly slow?
>
> When I say my first words to Eric, then God's reign will be here.[11]

Priest and author Henri J.M. Nouwen lost his mother to cancer in 1978. Throughout the busyness of his teaching and ministry, he realized he had not grieved. It was during a six-month retreat with the Trappist monks at the Abbey of the Genesee that he had the space and silence to grieve. During that time, less than a year after his mother's passing, he wrote a long letter to his father of which would later be published as "A Letter of Consolation." In seeking to bring comfort to his father, he ended up bringing comfort to himself as well. Below are two small excerpts of that letter.

> ...In her dying the real absurdity of death revealed itself to you. Only her death could really make you protest in your innermost being and make you cry out, "Why could our love not prevent her from dying?" Yet, the same love that reveals the absurdity of death also allows us to befriend death. The same love that forms the basis of our grief is also the basis of our hope; the same love that makes us cry out in pain also must enable us to develop a liberating intimacy with our own most basic brokenness. But our faith in him whose love overcame death and who rose from the grave on the third day converts this contradiction into a paradox, the most healing paradox of our existence...Many people seem never to befriend death and die as if they were losing a hopeless battle. But we do not have to share that sad fate. Mother's death can bring [freedom]; it can make us deeply aware that her love was a

---

11. Wolterstorff, *Lament for a Son*, 78.

reflection of a love that does not and cannot die—the love that we both will affirm again on Easter Sunday.[12]

Every time I look at that photograph of her grave, I experience again the new emotion that came to me after we buried her, an emotion so different from the emotion of seeing her again after a long absence, so different too from the emotion of watching her suffer and die. It is a new, very precious emotion. It is the emotion of a quiet, joyful waiting. Surely you know what I mean. There is a quiet contentment in this emotion. She has finished her life with us. She no longer has to suffer as we do; she no longer has to worry as we do; she no longer has to face the fear of death as we do. More than that, she will be spared the many anxieties and conflicts we still have to face. Nobody can harm her any more. We no longer have to protect her and be concerned about her health and safety. Oh, how we should love to have that concern again! But we have laid her to rest and she will not return. The rich soil in which we have buried her, the green hedges behind her grave, and the high lush trees around the small cemetery all create a feeling of safety, of being well received. But there is another side to this emotion. It includes waiting, quiet waiting. The solid, simple cross that stands above her grave speaks of something more than her death. Every time we go to that place, we sense that we are waiting, expecting, hoping. We wish to see her again and be with her once more, but we know that she has left us not to come back. At times, we wish to die and join her in death, but we know that we are called to live and to work on this earth. Our quiet, joyful waiting is much deeper than wishful thinking. It is waiting with the knowledge that love is stronger than death and that this truth will become visible to us. How? When? Where? These questions keep rushing into our impatient hearts. And yet, when we experience that quiet, joyful waiting, they cease troubling us and we feel that all is well.[13]

Professor and author Douglas Groothuis wrote the memoir *Walking Through Twilight: A Wife's Illness—A Philosopher's Lament*, while his beloved wife was battling dementia. He said he wrote it "to give a taste of what my lament is and then to explain how we may cope with such laments."[14]

---

12. Nouwen, *Letter of Consolation*, 33–34, 36.
13. Nouwen, *Letter of Consolation*, 80–82.
14. Groothuis, *Walking Through Twilight*, 8.

His thoughts and laments can bring comfort and solace to anyone slowly walking alongside a loved one who is battling illness. Hear his lament as he concludes his book:

> The twilight has been long for Becky and me. My last lament is that I have not done enough. I have not been enough. The voices say, "You should have spent more time with Becky. You should have pursued more doctors. You should have done more to keep Becky busy. You should have never raised your voice. You should not have depended so heavily on that friend. You should have. . . You should have not. . .
>
> But another voice says, "Yes and no." I can neither find nor write a roadmap for this death march into ever-deeper lament. My checklists are written in anguished ink. I cannot keep up. I am not a relativist, but there is no one right way to live through this. Each person with dementia is different, physically and psychologically; each caregiver is different, every situation is different. There is no roadmap, but there are detours to avoid; anger, selfishness, self-pity, rage, cowardice, dissipation, laziness, and the worst detour of all—deserting your post.
>
> But "love is as strong as death" (Song of Songs 8:6), and stronger. We know this because of an innocent man nailed to a Roman pike of shame, festooned by a dying criminal on each side. That young man died and was buried. Three days later, his tomb was emptied of death and he was found more alive than any of us are right now. These matchless and unmatchable events—written in books, but resident in reality—are my only hope in life and death, in Becky's life and in Becky's death. Jesus is Lord.[15]

In a written prayer, brilliant Christian philosopher and mathematician from the seventeenth century, Blaise Pascal, reflected to God what it means to suffer in different aspects of health, sickness, and the Christian life. He noted that when he was well, he often failed to acknowledge God, thank God, and use his health in service to God. When he became sick (he was inflicted with persistent illness and chronic pain), he prayed that God would use the sickness to strengthen his faith, which God so often does. Hear his words from the final section of this prayer:

15. Groothuis, *Walking Through Twilight*, 161–62.

Prayer, to Ask of God the Proper Use of Sickness, the final section XV

Blaise Pascal

Grant then, Lord, that such as I am I may conform myself to thy will; and that being sick as I am, I may glorify thee in my sufferings. Without them I could not arrive at glory; and thou, too, my Saviour, hast only wished to attain it through them. It was by the tokens of thy sufferings that thou wert recognized by thy disciples; and it is by sufferings also that thou wilt recognize thy disciples. Acknowledge me then for thy disciple in the evils which I endure both in my body and my mind, for the offences that I have committed. And since nothing is pleasing to God if it be not offered through thee, unite my will to thine, and my sorrows to those which thou hast suffered. Grant that mine may become thine. Unite me to thee; fill me with thyself and with thy Holy Spirit. Enter into my heart and soul, to bear in them my sufferings, and to continue to endure in me what remains to thee to suffer of thy passion, that thou mayest complete in thy members even the perfect consummation of thy body, so that being full of thee, it may no longer be that I live and suffer, but that it may be thou that livest and sufferest in me, O my Saviour! And that thus having some small part in thy sufferings, thou wilt fill me entirely with the glory that they have acquired for thee, in which thou wilt live with the Father and the Holy Spirit through ages upon ages. So be it.[16]

Horton Davies assembled and edited a resource of "Prayers of the Famous" throughout church history, titled *The Communion of Saints*. I have compiled some that I believe will be of great encouragement to you. My prayer as you read these is the same as his prayer in editing the volume: "It is imperative that we seek guidance and cheer from the noteworthy people here represented, who were burdened with great responsibilities that were lightened by prayer as they joined in the communion of saints."[17]

---

16. Pascal, "Prayer."
17. Davies, *Communion of Saints*, xiv.

PART TWO—DAVID

G.K. Chesterton (1874–1936)[18]

O God of earth and altar,
Bow down and hear our cry,
Our earthly rulers falter,
Our people drift and die;
The walls of gold entomb us,
The swords of scorn divide,
Take not your thunder from us,
But take away our pride!
From all that terror teaches,
From lies of tongue and pen,
From all the easy speeches,
That comfort cruel men,
From sale and profanation
Of honor and the sword,
From sleep and from damnation,
Deliver us, good Lord.

Søren Kierkegaard (1813–1855)[19]

O Lord, calm the waves of this heart; calm its tempests. Calm yourself, O my soul, so that the divine can act in you. Calm yourself, O my soul, so that God is able to repose in you, so that his peace may cover you. Yes, Father in heaven, often have we found that the world cannot give us peace, O but make us feel that you are able to give peace; let us know the truth of your promise: that the whole world may not be able to take away your peace.

William Sloane Coffin, Jr. (1924–2006)[20]

We come to you in penitence, confessing our sins: the vows we have forgotten, the opportunities we have let slip, the excuses whereby we have sought to deceive ourselves and you. Forgive us that we talk so much and are silent so seldom; that we are in such constant motion and are so rarely still; that we depend so implicitly on the effectiveness of our organizations and so little on

---

18. Davies, *Communion of Saints*, 24.
19. Davies, *Communion of Saints*, 91.
20. Davies, *Communion of Saints*, 93.

the power of your Spirit. Teach us to wait upon you, that we may renew our strength, mount up with wings as eagles, run and not be weary, walk and not faint.

John Calvin (1509–1564)[21]

Grant, almighty God, that, since the dullness and harshness of our flesh is so great that it is needful for us in various ways to be afflicted, we may patiently bear your chastisement, and under a deep feeling of sorrow flee to your mercy displayed to us in Christ; and that, not depending upon the earthly blessings of this perishable life, but relying only upon your Word, we may go forward in the course of our calling; until at length we are gathered to that blessed rest which is laid up for us in heaven; through Jesus Christ our Lord.

Teilhard de Chardin (1881–1955)[22]

When the signs of age begin to mark my body (and still more when they touch my mind); when the ill that is to diminish me or carry me off strikes from without or is born within me; when the painful moment comes in which I suddenly awaken to the fact that I am ill or growing old; and above all at that last moment when I feel I am losing hold of myself and am absolutely passive within the hands of the great unknown forces that have formed me; in all those dark moments, O God, grant that I may understand that it is you (provided only my faith is strong enough) who are painfully parting the fibers of my being in order to penetrate to the very marrow of my substance and bear me away within yourself.

In 1893, Mary W. Tileston selected and arranged prayers spanning fourteen centuries and titled it *Great Souls at Prayer*. The small book has had a large and continued impact, as it has been reprinted over fifty times. Each entry only simply includes the authors' name, with no backstories,

---

21. Davies, *Communion of Saints*, 133.
22. Davies, *Communion of Saints*, 137.

though some content can be assumed. I have compiled the ones below that I think will be of most service to voicing your heart's cry.

Thomas à Kempis[23]

In Thee, O Lord God, I place my whole hope and refuge; on Thee I rest all my tribulation and anguish; for I find all to be weak and inconstant, whatsoever I behold out of Thee. For many friends cannot profit, nor strong helpers assist, nor the books of the learned afford comfort, nor any place, however retired and lovely, give shelter, unless Thou Thyself dost assist, strengthen, console, instruct, and guard us. For all things that seem to belong to the attainment of peace and felicity, without Thee, are nothing, and do bring in truth no felicity at all. Thou therefore art the Fountain of all that is good; and to hope in Thee above all things, is the strongest comfort of Thy servants. To Thee, therefore, do I lift up mine eyes; in Thee, my God, the Father of mercies, do I put my trust—Amen.

John Woolman (1720–1772)[24]

O Lord, my God! The amazing horrors of darkness were gathered round me, and covered me all over, and I saw no way to go forth; I felt the depth and extent of the misery of my fellow-creatures separated from the Divine harmony, and it was heavier than I could bear, and I was crushed down under it; I lifted up my hand, I stretched out my arm, but there was none to help me; I looked round about, and was amazed. In the depths of misery, O Lord, I remembered that Thou art omnipotent; that I had called Thee Father; and I felt that I loved Thee, and I was made quiet in my will, and I waited for deliverance from Thee. Thou hadst pity upon me, when no man could help me; I saw that meekness under suffering was showed to us in the most affecting example of Thy Son, and Thou taughtest me to follow Him, and I said, "Thy will, O Father, be done!"

---

23. Tileston, *Great Souls at Prayer*, 158.
24. Tileston, *Great Souls at Prayer*, 245.

Henry W. Foote[25]

Holy Father, whose chosen way of manifesting Thyself to Thy children is by the discipline of trial and pain, we rejoice that we can turn to Thee in the midst of great anxiety, and commit all our troubles to Thy sure help. As Thou art with us in the sunlight, oh, be Thou with us in the cloud. In the path by which Thou guidest us, though it be through desert and stormy sea, suffer not our faith to fail, but sustain us by Thy near presence, and let the comforts which are in Jesus Christ fill our hearts with peace. And, O God, grant that the fiery trial which trieth us may not be in vain, but may lead us to a cheerful courage, and a holy patience; and let the patience have her perfect work, that we may be perfect and entire, wanting nothing, wholly consecrate to Thee, through Jesus Christ our Lord—Amen.

J.F. Stark[26]

Lord! When I am in sorrow I think on Thee. Listen to the cry of my heart, and my sorrowful complaint. Yet, O Father, I would not prescribe to Thee when and how Thy help should come. I will willingly tarry for the hour which Thou Thyself hast appointed for my relief. Meanwhile strengthen me by Thy Holy Spirit; strengthen my faith, my hope, my trust; give me patience and resolution to bear my trouble; and let me at last behold the time when Thou wilt make me glad with Thy grace. Ah, my Father! Never yet hast Thou forsaken Thy children, forsake me not. Ever dost Thou give gladness unto the sorrowful, O give it now unto me. Always dost Thou relieve me too, when and where and how Thou wilt. Unto Thy wisdom, love, and goodness, I leave it utterly—Amen.

Thomas à Kempis[27]

O Lord my God, be no Thou far from me; my God, have regard to help me; for there have risen up against me sundry thoughts, and great fears, afflicting my soul. How shall I pass through unhurt? How shall I break them to pieces? This is my hope, my one only

---

25. Tileston, *Great Souls at Prayer*, 273.
26. Tileston, *Great Souls at Prayer*, 316.
27. Tileston, *Great Souls at Prayer*, 350.

consolation, to flee unto Thee in every tribulation, to trust in Thee, to call upon Thee from my inmost heart, and to wait patiently for Thy consolation—Amen.

S. Scheretz (1584–1639)[28]

Ah, God! Behold my grief and care. Fain would I serve Thee with a glad and cheerful countenance, but I cannot do it. However much I fight and struggle against my sadness, I am too weak for this sore conflict. Help me in my weakness, O Thou mighty God! And give me Thy Holy Spirit to refresh and comfort me in my sorrow. Amid all my fears and griefs I yet know that I am Thine in life and death, and that nothing can really part me from Thee; neither things present, nor things to come, neither trial, nor fear, nor pain. And therefore, O Lord, I will still trust in Thy grace. Thou wilt not send me away unheard. Sooner or later Thou wilt lift this burden from my heart, and put a new song in my lips; and I will praise Thy goodness, and thank and serve Thee here and for evermore—Amen.

I hope you have seen through these real-life laments how God can use even the hardest moments of your life to help someone else through theirs. You do not have to publish your laments for God to hear them, or even write them down. But take time today to express your honest, heartfelt cries to God. He hears.

28. Tileston, *Great Souls at Prayer*, 364.

PART THREE

JESUS THE SUFFERING SERVANT
Our Place in God's Grand Redemptive Story

Chapter Nine

Recognizing He is Enough
The Battle of Expectations

Ezekiel 37:24-25

[24] "My servant David shall be king over them, and they shall all have one shepherd. They shall walk in my rules and be careful to obey my statutes. [25] They shall dwell in the land that I gave to my servant Jacob, where your fathers lived. They and their children and their children's children shall dwell there forever, and David my servant shall be their prince forever.

THROUGHOUT AND FOLLOWING THE time of King David, promises were made by God, and expectations were set by his people. That's what we do when a promise is made, right? We have certain expectations. The thing is though, expectations are not always accurate. One of the first things my wife and I learned in preparing for marriage was to get rid of all expectations, though in our self-centered brokenness we have often failed at this. The reason we are to remove expectations is because often times they are false expectations. They are not expectations we should place on someone else.

Now there are many noble expectations we should set in marriage, such as fidelity, love, provision, and seeking the welfare of the other, to name a few. But the expectations I am talking about flow from personal preference, not objective standards. Like when I respond to my wife with, "Yes, I will take out the trash." In my mind that means I will take out the trash the next time I get up to go to the kitchen or before I go to bed or the day after tomorrow (oops!). But when I tell her that I will take out the trash, she has a completely different expectation. She expects me to get up and take out the trash right now (and maybe her expectation is justified knowing I sometimes forget). Thankfully, we have both learned a lot over our last decade of marriage on how to communicate our expectations and show grace when they are not met. But hopefully you get my point. When promises are made, expectations are automatically set, whether they are right or not.

Going back to King David, God made a promise that he would have a descendant to sit on his throne forever.[1] David was the greatest king Israel had ever known and victorious in almost every battle he led. So naturally with this promise came the expectation that the nation of Israel would be secure for all time. But there was a condition within that promise. If the kings who followed David failed to honor and obey the Lord, God would allow Israel to go through hardship and exile due to their disobedience. However, he would still keep his promise. And generations later, that is exactly where the Israelites found themselves, suffering in exile. But there they remembered the promises God had made. They remembered God saying King David's throne would be established forever. And they knew God had kept all his promises before. So they waited. And hoped. And waited. And hoped. And waited. And hoped. They were waiting with hopeful anticipation for a king to come and rescue them from their suffering. But they didn't realize they were waiting with a false expectation.

God's people wanted "a king on a throne full of power, with a sword in his fist,"[2] and their hope for such a conquering king who would bring them back their Promised Land was justified. But *God knew better. God intended better. God was bringing better.* They were hoping for another king like David, but God was planning on coming himself to fight the battle man couldn't. Every geographical conquest that God had ever provided for his

---

1. 2 Sam 7:16.
2. These are lyrics from Andrew Peterson's song "So Long Moses."

people was going to pale in comparison to the conquest that God taking on human flesh came to fulfill: the conquest of the human heart.

Jesus came to rule hearts, not land. And this terrain was in far worse shape than any Promised Land. There was bloodshed, as in any battle. But this blood wasn't shed by the soldiers or the enemies. This blood was shed by the King. He was coming to suffer, and it was going to hurt. But he was coming to win. Jesus's coming brought about far more than a military conquest ever could. And he would defeat a far worse enemy than any foreign army—the enemy of sin and death.

The promise fulfilled by God was far grander than anyone could imagine when he first uttered those words to David centuries earlier. He knew what his people needed. God in human flesh, in unglamorous glory, in suffering servitude coming to save the souls of his people for generations and generations to come. God prophesied this.[3] It was his plan all along. His people didn't need a great conquering king to rule and reign for them. They needed God to rule and reign in their hearts and lives. God, the one true King, was coming to do battle. But in order to do so, he would have to draw near.

Instead of coming on a horse with a sword in his fist like other conquering kings did, the Creator of life was born as a baby into the world he once held in his hands, which brings us to the first Christmas passage in the Bible. No, it's not found in the prophecies of Isaiah or in Matthew, although those are great Christmas passages, too. It's found all the way back at the beginning of the world, directly in the middle of the dark hopelessness of the very first sin. Grab your Bible and turn to Genesis 3.

The First Prophecy of Jesus

What we see in Genesis 1 and 2 is that God, in his sovereignty, created everything good. We were created for beauty and enjoyment of life and freedom and intimacy with God. Eden is our proto-Promised Land, and in this land, God made Adam and Eve free creatures knowing that they could freely love him. Knowing he could fully demonstrate his love for them. But also knowing they were going to rebel against him. I believe God knew Adam and Eve would disobey before he created them. He didn't want them to disobey, but I don't think he was surprised when they did and caused sin to stain the once perfect world he had made.

3. Isaiah 53.

PART THREE—JESUS THE SUFFERING SERVANT

Adam and Eve had everything they could ever need in the Garden of Eden, but they believed the lie that it wasn't enough. That God was holding out on them. That they knew better than God what was good for them. When Adam and Eve disobeyed God's orders to not eat from one particular tree, even though they were completely free to eat from every other tree, their intimacy with God was broken. Immediately after falling into sin, Adam and Eve hid from the God they once walked with. I'm not a huge fan of walking, but my wife is, and usually when we have that time together, we talk as we walk. It was the same with Adam, Eve, and God. Daily they had intimate fellowship with one another in the garden. But when Adam and Eve sinned, there were no more walks with God or talking to him face to face, because a perfect, holy God cannot be in fellowship with an imperfect, sinful man. Sin always separates us from God's presence.

But let me clarify, it wasn't God who ran away from the relationship with his creation when sin entered the world. It was Adam and Eve who ran and hid from their Creator. God never pushes us away, even in our sin and brokenness. It is you and I who go and hide. As the great hymn "Come, Thou Fount of Every Blessing" says, "Prone to wander, Lord I feel it, prone to leave the God I love." We are all prone to wander because it is in our flesh. We are born into this sin that Adam and Eve initiated. And sin would continue creating a divide between God and man throughout history.

But what we see from the beginning, from the very first sin, is that God never intended for us to stay separated. He longed to be near Adam and Eve again. He longed for intimacy with them, walking and talking with his creation again. God could have wiped out Adam and Eve and started all over. He could have created robots to follow his every order without second thought. But instead of crushing Adam and Eve or wiping out their existence, God made a promise to one day rescue them. He was going to make a way. He was going to *be* the way. It is in this promise that we see the first prophecy of Jesus:

> [14] The Lord God said to the serpent, "Because you have done this, cursed are you above all livestock and above all beasts of the field; on your belly you shall go, and dust you shall eat all the days of your life. [15] I will put enmity between you and the woman, and between your offspring and her offspring; he shall bruise your head, and you shall bruise his heel."[4]

---

4. Gen 3:14–15.

This is called the *protoevangelium*. The first gospel. The first good news. You might be wondering how there could be good news in the middle of a curse. But amidst the brokenness of sin, the glory and hope of God's great love lit up the darkness. The curse wasn't simply a curse but also a promise. A promise that the serpent would one day be bruised, or crushed, by man. I kind of see this as pay back to Satan for tricking Eve into sin (plus, I am terrified of snakes and wouldn't be upset if they were all crushed). But in that promise God says the woman's offspring would be crushed as well. Where's the hope in that?

Let's think about this for a second. The offspring of a woman is a baby. And what do we celebrate at Christmas? God coming into the world as a baby! Who was this baby's mother? Mary. Surely God had Mary in mind at this moment in Genesis knowing she would carry *his* offspring. So the seed of the woman the curse was talking about would miraculously be God himself. God loved Adam and Eve so much that he wrote himself into the very curse he was placing on them. He would go to such unimaginable lengths of love to be crushed on a cross in order to crush our brokenness and heal our intimacy with him. Though that day in the Garden of Eden everything changed, God promised that he himself would draw near to restore what sin had broken. This is why he prophecied that he would be called Immanuel (*God with us*),[5] and the virgin would conceive *him*.[6] He was coming to fight, and he was willing to die on the battlefield to fix our fractured intimacy with him.

When I think of battles, I cannot help but think of conquering kings. It comes with the territory. Well, it comes with the conquest of territory, which is what battles in the Promised Land literally are. So if our Promised Land is equal to the abundant Christian life now and forevermore, then how can we fully attain it? How can that territory become ours? The same way conquest battles happened in the olden days—a king must fight on behalf of his people.

I believe God had it in his heart before Genesis 1 that he was going to come and suffer for us to demonstrate the magnificence of his love for us. He was going to die in battle in order to give us our Promised Land, the abundant Christian life that can only be found in him. There is no greater love than the sacrifice of Jesus. Even amidst all the evil and suffering that sin has brought, it is but a light and momentary affliction against the

5. Matt 1:23.
6. Isa 7:14.

eternity Christ has bought. Yes, he promised pain and suffering for Adam and Eve because of their sin, but he also promised redemption. God had planned from the beginning what would take place thousands of years later. He knew there would be battles in between. He knew there would be suffering in between. He knew it would be hard and people would grow tired of waiting. But he would keep making a way. He would keep fighting. To fulfill his promise to rescue them. To show them he has been and always will be enough.

The Promise of God's Presence

From Genesis 3 on, throughout all of Biblical history, God kept reminding his people what he started in Eden. He kept reminding them of his promise. He kept reminding them of his presence. He kept reminding them he was fixing the fractured intimacy they longed for. He was still with his people, even though they could not see or talk with him face to face.

We see over and over again throughout the Bible God constantly reminding his people that he is with them, that his presence is all they need. Because he is enough. One of the most beautiful and reoccurring promises in the Bible is, "I will not leave you nor forsake you."[7] God's presence was promised to Moses when God gave him the charge to lead his people out of slavery in Egypt. It was emphatically communicated to Joshua when God told him to go and conquer the Promised Land. We see countless Old Testament saints trust God through hard situations because they knew God was with them. Surely every time God repeated those words, he thought of the not-so-far-away day when he would lie down in a manger, having put on flesh, to dwell with his people. He certainly would not leave nor forsake them then. And he has not left or forsaken us since.

As was stated earlier, it was God's plan from the beginning to rescue his people. He knew that his creatures would sin against him. He knew he would have to make a way for their redemption through his son, Jesus. He knew it would cost him his life, but it would be worth it to show them the greatest love imaginable. Every book of the Bible points to this grand redemptive narrative. And every battle in the Old Testament points to a greater battle that is to be won through Jesus. I love how Sally Llyod-Jones poignantly writes it in *The Jesus Storybook Bible*, "Every story whispers his

---

7. Deut 31:6; Josh 1:9; Heb 13:5.

name." That is, the name of Jesus. The name that means "the Lord saves," because that is indeed what he was coming to do.

Jesus is a form of the Hebrew name Joshua, which means "God is salvation." Therefore, the name Jesus carries with it all the reminders of God's past faithfulness through every battle Joshua fought in the Promised Land. Jesus is also a name that comes from the lineage of David, a man after God's own heart, who trusted God amidst much adversity. Jesus is the name for God in the flesh. Amidst his people. For his people. Bringing them to himself. Every battle, from the first mention of conflict in Genesis 3 to the prophecies in Isaiah 53 to thousands of years later in Matthew 1, was working its way to this moment when God would put on flesh.

However when Jesus came, many people didn't believe his story. They didn't trust him to be the long-expected Messiah they had been waiting for. He didn't meet their standards of what they thought king should be. He didn't look like royalty. He didn't act like a warrior ready to fight. His speech and habits and eating with sinners and calling out the Pharisees and talking of a kingdom that wasn't in Jerusalem made them turn away and ignore the door to freedom that was right in front of them. In their minds, Jesus wasn't enough. They wanted more. And many would die holding onto their expectations and waiting for another king to fit their criteria rather than accept the one true King who had come to rescue them.

Don't we do the same thing?

We often look at our life and think, "God, this isn't what I was expecting." The hardship, the suffering, the pain we have to deal with on a daily basis, whether it's from our own flesh or other people around us or circumstances beyond our control. Often we lose sight of how God could be working those things for our good. So we count him out. We ignore him. We assume he isn't working our situation for good or is far off and unaware of what we are even going through. Maybe we question if he even exists at all. Or if we do believe he exists, we question if he's really good. So we turn to other things besides God to satisfy us. To fill that empty void. But no amount of love, drugs, alcohol, sexual fulfillment, material gain, work achievement, familial bond, fame, or anything else we are longing for in this life can satisfy us like God alone can. Sometimes the whole point of suffering is to strip us away from all the things we hold dear until all that's left is Jesus. That's when we realize he is enough. And when we look to him for who he is and not who we expect him to be, that's when we will find he is greater than anything we could ask for or imagine.

PART THREE—JESUS THE SUFFERING SERVANT

I love what Pastor John R. Claypool has to say about expectation of God regarding our suffering in his book *Tracks of a Fellow Struggler*, written from sermons he preached after losing his eight-year-old daughter to leukemia. In light of the verse in Isa 40:31, "but they who wait for the Lord shall renew their strength; they shall mount up with wings like eagles; they shall run and not be weary; they shall walk and not faint," here is what Claypool has to say:

> Therefore, I was not disappointed [in God]. At the bottom of the darkness, my faith truly did make a difference. Why? Partly because I did not erect false expectations; I let God be God and give me what God willed to give and what was appropriate. God gave power to me, the faint; for me, the one who had no might, God increased my strength.
>
> Well, that is how it was, and here I am this morning—sad, brokenhearted, still bearing in my spirit the wounds of the darkness. I confess to you honestly that I have no wings with which to fly or even any legs on which to run—but listen, by the grace of God, *I am still on my feet!* I have not fainted yet. I have not exploded in the anger of presumption, nor have I keeled over into the paralysis of despair. All I am doing is walking and not fainting, hanging in there, enduring with patience what I cannot change but have to bear. . .
>
> And who knows, if I am willing to accept this gift, and just hang in there and not cop out, maybe the day will come that Laura Lue and I can run again and not be weary, and that we may even soar some day, and rise up with wings as eagles! But until then—to walk and not faint, that is enough. O God, that is enough![8]

God is always enough for us. His plans and purposes are far-reaching from eternity and into eternity. Yet our lives are finite, and our vision tends to be near sighted. We lose sight of his promises. We place our expectations above his sovereignty and goodness. We run and hide from God. We kick and scream for more when his presence is already enough. And when our expectations of who we think he should be or what he should do for us are not met, we question if God is really good and in control.

Any time I write someone a note to tell them I am praying for them, I purposefully seek to remind them of this fact: "God is good and in control." But so often within our fractured minds, that statement seems contradictory. If God is truly in control and we find ourselves in a hard situation, then

---

8. Claypool, *Tracks of a Fellow Struggler*, 43–44.

it seems to us he is not good. But that is a false expectation that we have placed on God. Amidst every single aspect of our lives, God is good and in control. Those are not mutually exclusive claims. They are intrinsically compatible truths about our King who humbled himself in love, taking the form of a servant, and becoming obedient to death on a cross.[9]

Because we can trace God's plan of redemption from the garden to the incarnation, we can know that nothing has happened in this evil world outside of God's control and nothing will happen unless it goes through God first. Since the beginning of creation, God has been setting his plan in motion to bring an end to evil and suffering by sacrificing his own son, Jesus. And since God has been faithful in the past, we can trust him to be faithful no matter what the future holds.

So even if your situation feels unbearable and out of control, know that God is working amidst any battles you face. God promises to be with you wherever you are, giving you strength to face whatever hardship you're in. He is Immanuel. God with you. Dwelling with you. Walking with you. Talking with you. Singing over you. He is celebrating every triumph and consoling every loss. He is holding you up when you cannot stand and pushing you from behind when you cannot run. He is encouraging you when your doubts are loud, and he is near to you when your heart is broken. He is speaking words of wisdom when folly is enticing, and he's giving you words to speak when you're standing up alone for him. He knows your pain, your struggle, your joys, and your desires. He provides your every need, knows you better than you know yourself, and fights battles for you that you could never win on your own. He knows what lies before you, and he is not afraid. Therefore, you should not be either. He promises you peace and hope and joy and love. He says you have no need to worry. No need to fear. No need to doubt. Because he is near. He is right where you left him, waiting with open arms to show you more of himself that is greater than you can imagine. He might not be who you are expecting but he is exactly who you need. Will you turn to him and trust him to be enough for you today?

---

9. Phil 2:7–8.

Chapter Ten

Overcoming Your Lineage
The Battle of Legacy

Galatians 4:4–7

⁴ But when the fullness of time had come, God sent forth his Son, born of woman, born under the law, ⁵ to redeem those who were under the law, so that we might receive adoption as sons. ⁶ And because you are sons, God has sent the Spirit of his Son into our hearts, crying, "Abba! Father!" ⁷ So you are no longer a slave, but a son, and if a son, then an heir through God.

YOU HAVE PROBABLY EXPERIENCED it. I know I have. When something terrible or hard to process has taken place, the most difficult thing to do is turn off your mind from the what-ifs and if-onlys and go to sleep. The easiest thing to do is stay busy because when your head hits that pillow, the lights go out, and you're alone with your thoughts, the quiet always sounds so loud. Your mind needs rest, but the problem is stuck on repeat and the channel can't be changed. It's why so many people turn to alcohol or sleeping aids when going through hard times. They can't be alone with their thoughts. If all of us have experienced it, Joseph, the father of Jesus, likely did, too.

Can you imagine what Joseph must have felt when he found out the woman he loved was pregnant, and there was no way the child was his? Devastation. Betrayal. Shame. He was a good man. An honorable man. But now his fiancé was pregnant by someone else. A tidal wave of thoughts—anger, fears, what-ifs, how-could-shes, what-do-I-do-nows, and deep, lingering sadness—surely swept him off his feet and pummeled him around and around until he could hardly breathe, grasping for air. Still, amidst his suffering, his character shone through. He could have sought public humiliation and punishment for Mary, but he resolved to divorce her quietly. He still cared for her, even though he knew he had to move on with his life. He didn't know how, but he would figure it out. As he laid his head on his pillow, his mind couldn't stop. If only he could fall asleep.

By the grace of God, he did. And while he slept, he dreamed.

What happens next in the story of Joseph has become so repetitive that we tend to miss it when we read the Christmas story every year. Just as you naturally tune out the sound of a fan, we have in many ways tuned out the wonder of God's redemptive plan in the advent, or coming, of Jesus. While Joseph was sleeping, an angel comes to him in his dream, tells him to take Mary as his wife, that the baby is conceived from the Holy Spirit, and that he should name him Jesus because he will save his people from their sins. You've heard it all before, right? But what the angel says and who he says it to is the fulfillment of every battle and promise made in the Old Testament, flowing all the way back from the Garden of Eden. The angel confirms to Joseph in his dream that this is the long-awaited Messiah, the fulfillment of the prophecies from long ago, the promise that God would dwell with his people, as we learned in the last chapter. It was all part of God's great plan of salvation, and it was unfolding before Joseph's very eyes.

The Importance of Lineage

When reading the first page of our New Testament, we come face to face with the lineage of Jesus. What may seem boring and odd to some, is actually full of power, faithfulness, sovereignty, and salvation. The lineage in Matthew 1 is a concentrated summation of God's redemptive narrative that had been played out since his initial covenant with his people in Genesis 12. The first words of Matthew 1 read, "The book of the genealogy of Jesus Christ, the son of David, the son of Abraham."

PART THREE—JESUS THE SUFFERING SERVANT

God had promised Abraham that his progeny would outnumber the stars in the sky, even though he was old and could not have any children. And God was faithful to his covenant. In Matthew 1 we see a lineage that starts with the old barren couple at the head and goes on and on. God not only made a covenant with Abraham, but also with Abraham's descendent, King David. In 2 Samuel 7, the prophet Nathan speaks these words from the Lord to David, "Your house and your kingdom shall be made sure forever before me. Your throne shall be established forever."

The angel of the Lord that appeared in Joseph's dream is talking to the descendent of David, telling him—Joseph—that he is to name his child Jesus, because he will save his people from their sins. Most women have a say in what they will name their own children, but Jesus' name was determined before the foundations of the world, and God chose to reveal that name to Joseph. What we see in the genealogy of Matthew 1 is God's faithful covenant with both Abraham and David coming to fruition in grand fashion, culminating with Joseph, the earthly father of Jesus.

But not everyone in Jesus' lineage lined up with the godly character of Abraham, David, or Joseph. When tracing the narrative throughout the genealogy of Jesus, we see people either fighting for God or fighting against him. Some of them passed down faith and courage, while others passed down idolatry and fear. Many more kings did what was evil in the sight of the Lord than did what was good and right and true in the eyes of the Lord. Joseph came from this line. An impure lineage. A lineage that neither trusted God nor lived for his glory. But God's redemption story is greater than any weakness of mankind. When the angel is talking to Joseph, telling him that the Messiah has come and that Joseph should give him the name Jesus, he is saying that God is going to fulfill his every promise even though his people and his family haven't measured up.

You may have a tainted lineage, too. Oftentimes some of our deepest struggles and sufferings in life come from the family line we are born into. Our genetic disposition sometimes imposes certain habits, temptations, and sins that we feel like we cannot shake. Often we tend to follow in the footsteps of our family members, sometimes spanning generations, just like several of the kings in Jesus' lineage did. But it only takes one to break the sinful pattern. Because when we are reborn into Christ's family, we become a new creation.[1] We take on a new identity and a new family name. And

---

1. 2 Cor 5:17.

even though we are still sinners, we are no longer under the bondage of our family's tainted legacy.

What's In a Name

I don't think it is coincidence that the angel came and gave Joseph instructions on what to name the child Mary had conceived. Joseph may have seemed like a nobody, but he belonged to a somebody. When Joseph is lying his head on his pillow, receiving the vision and announcement from the angel, all of God's promises were continuing to be fulfilled since Joseph belonged to the lineage of David. I'm not sure if he quite understood in that moment the significance and magnitude his obedience would have in the grand redemptive narrative. But Joseph did exactly as the angel had said. He took Mary as his wife, and when she gave birth, he named the baby Jesus.

As we learned in the previous chapter, the name of Jesus was a form of the name of Joshua.[2] Not only was there history of battles won behind the name of Jesus in the same Promised Land where Joshua won many battles, but there was foresight into the greatest battle that was to be won for all time. Jesus, meaning "the Lord Saves," was coming to save his people from their sins. In Bible times, names were not given to children arbitrarily. They meant something. Behind the name of this baby was a history of God's redemption. Behind this name of Jesus is not only the promise of salvation but also the evidence of salvation. Behind the name of this baby was battle after battle after battle after battle that would be fought, and victory after victory after victory after victory that would be won. Behind the name of this baby was the fulfillment of the Promised Land. The kingdom of heaven really was coming to earth. It wasn't a military conquest that this King was coming to bring. He was coming to rule a greater kingdom. He was coming to be the Savior and Ruler of our hearts.

Just as Joshua had participated in the Passover meal that the Israelites celebrated every year, Jesus was coming to be the Passover lamb for us. When the Lord spared all of the firstborn males in Egypt who had slaughtered a lamb and spread the blood over the door post of their homes, God was pointing to the day that he would come as a firstborn male, to be slaughtered as a lamb, so his blood could be spread over the lives of all who

---

2. McGee, *Joshua and Judges*, x.

would put their faith in him—a once-for-all sacrifice to cover the sins of the world.

All this grand narrative is wrapped up in this tiny little scene of Joseph's dream that we so often overlook in the Christmas story. That is why it is important to note whom the angel is coming to and what the angel is proclaiming. God was entering the world. He was putting on flesh. And he was coming as a little baby, Mary and Joseph's baby, to be named Jesus because he was coming to save. It was all for a purpose. God did not just arbitrarily decide to come to earth and one day think, "Oh, it might be neat if I come as a baby!" No, it was purposeful. It was planned. He was coming to do battle. He was coming to crush the head of that ancient serpent. But as was planned and made known from the beginning that he was going to be crushed as well.

God as a Baby

Have you ever wondered why God came as a baby? Of all ways to come into the world, why that way? If you had such power that you created the entirety of existence by the word of your mouth, why would you choose to become so small? Why not come in that same power of the cosmic beginning of creation with a bang of "let there be light"? There are many reasons why actually. For starters, the original prophecy in Gen 3:15 had to do with the "seed" of the woman, which we know is referring to a baby. Whether we understand why or not, it is clear that it was God's plan from the beginning to become small. But I believe another grander reason God came as a baby has to do with our sin.

One of my favorite Christmas passages is not found in any of the gospels. It is actually from the apostle Paul in Gal 4:4–7, at the beginning of this chapter.

One of the reasons Jesus came as a baby, according to this passage, is to be born under the law in order to redeem those who were under the law. What does it mean to be under the law? First, it reveals to us the plight we are in. The true battle that we fight every day is that we live under the dominion of sin.[3] It is as much a part of our heritage as the eye color, nose shape, or blood type we have. We are all born as sinners. And the one grand purpose of the law is to reveal our sin. Let's pause and read how the apostle Paul explains the law and sin in Rom 7:7–25:

3. Schreiner, *Galatians*, 271.

⁷ What then shall we say? That the law is sin? By no means! Yet if it had not been for the law, I would not have known sin. For I would not have known what it is to covet if the law had not said, "You shall not covet." ⁸ But sin, seizing an opportunity through the commandment, produced in me all kinds of covetousness. For apart from the law, sin lies dead. ⁹ I was once alive apart from the law, but when the commandment came, sin came alive and I died. ¹⁰ The very commandment that promised life proved to be death to me. ¹¹ For sin, seizing an opportunity through the commandment, deceived me and through it killed me. ¹² So the law is holy, and the commandment is holy and righteous and good.

¹³ Did that which is good, then, bring death to me? By no means! It was sin, producing death in me through what is good, in order that sin might be shown to be sin, and through the commandment might become sinful beyond measure. ¹⁴ For we know that the law is spiritual, but I am of the flesh, sold under sin. ¹⁵ For I do not understand my own actions. For I do not do what I want, but I do the very thing I hate. ¹⁶ Now if I do what I do not want, I agree with the law, that it is good. ¹⁷ So now it is no longer I who do it, but sin that dwells within me. ¹⁸ For I know that nothing good dwells in me, that is, in my flesh. For I have the desire to do what is right, but not the ability to carry it out. ¹⁹ For I do not do the good I want, but the evil I do not want is what I keep on doing. ²⁰ Now if I do what I do not want, it is no longer I who do it, but sin that dwells within me.

²¹ So I find it to be a law that when I want to do right, evil lies close at hand. ²² For I delight in the law of God, in my inner being, ²³ but I see in my members another law waging war against the law of my mind and making me captive to the law of sin that dwells in my members. ²⁴ Wretched man that I am! Who will deliver me from this body of death? ²⁵ Thanks be to God through Jesus Christ our Lord! So then, I myself serve the law of God with my mind, but with my flesh I serve the law of sin.

In these verses we see there are two laws at work. There is the law of sin, and there is the law of God (vs 25). Jesus came to deliver us from the law of sin. This causes Paul, and hopefully you, to say, "Thanks be to God through Jesus Christ our Lord!" But also Paul still understands there is an inward battle we continue to fight now. Though we understand the law of God is good and right, and we may even delight in it (vs 22), we still dwell under the law of sin. We still deal with our sinful heritage on a daily basis. We desire to do good, but the war is always being waged within us. There is a constant internal battle that we can never fully win, and it's agonizing.

PART THREE—JESUS THE SUFFERING SERVANT

It's not so with Jesus, though. And that's why Jesus came to do battles in the Promised Land, to defeat our sin. Hear what theologian Thomas R. Schreiner says about this Galatians passage and what it means for us:

> Those who live under the law. . .live under the dominion of sin. Jesus, however, is the exception that proves the rule. He is the true offspring of Abraham (3:16), the true Israel (Ex 4:22), the true Son of God. He lived obediently to God's law, whereas all others violated God's will. As the one who lived under the law, he took the curse of the law on himself (3:13) so that he could liberate and free those who were captivated by the power of sin.[4]

Galatians 4:4–7 takes the application even further for us. Because the Son was born under the law to redeem those who are under the law, those who place their faith in him are adopted into God's family as sons and daughters (vs 5). We are made children of God through the Son of God. We are freed and provided for and given a home and nurtured and loved. That's one reason Jesus came as a baby, to fulfil the law and make us family, but also to demonstrate for us what it is like to be a child of God.

One of the greatest joys of my life was when we adopted our little girl. You heard me share in an earlier chapter about the devastation my wife and I felt when the door closed on our plan to adopt from Ethiopia. But we kept pursuing the calling we felt God had placed on our hearts and prayed for the child we believed God had for our family. And after nearly ten years of waiting (off and on through different organizations), we finally got the call one morning that we had been chosen for a little girl in our state who was two weeks old and getting discharged that day. We rushed to get clothes out of the attic, clean the diaper bag out, and drop our kids off with the grandparents. We drove four hours to the hospital and bought a new car seat on the way. Two hours later, we walked out of the hospital with our daughter in our hands and drove four hours back home, exhausted but in awe of the gift we had been given. It was a whirlwind of a day, but I wouldn't change it for anything.

I have heard many people who have both biological and adopted kids say that there is nothing different in the way they love their children who came from their own flesh and blood and their children who were adopted. I completely agree. The only difference is the choice you make in choosing to parent a child whom you are under no biological obligation to. You take them in. You provide for them. You pour yourself out for them just like you

---

4. Schreiner, *Galatians*, 270.

do your other kids. You fill out lots of paperwork, pay lots of money, and go through a long legal process of changing their last name so everyone knows they belong to your family. It's not always easy, but what a privilege it is to make that choice. Even though our daughter was exposed to more darkness in the two weeks of her life before we met her than I have been in my entire lifetime, she now has a new family legacy. She has the stability of a family who chose her, wants her, loves her, and accepts her for who she is, and hopefully she will pass that along to her kids and grandkids one day.

I think God came as a baby because he wanted to show us we were chosen for his family. He didn't come for us because he had to. He came for us because he wanted to. He wanted us. He chose to adopt us and would go through all the hardship again if that meant that we would get to spend eternity with him. He chose to take on our sins and endure our punishment for us so that we could receive adoption as his sons and daughters. So we could share in his inheritance of eternal life because we now bear the name of Jesus. That is the kind of love God demonstrated to us.

Sharing Sorrows and Fulfilling Promises

Next time you're suffering, next time you're doubting, next time you're fighting against your flesh, remember who Jesus is and how he came. Jesus is the fulfillment of the promise of Immanuel, "God with us."[5] He came as a baby, born into the same cruel world as us, tempted with the same fleshly sin as us, and suffered more than any of us ever could, all to show he understands our plight.

The almighty was made helpless so he could show us where our help comes from. The one of whom all things depend on for their sustained existence was made dependent on a teenage girl. The one who created the cosmos was confined to the arms of his mother and adoptive father. The one who spoke trees into existence on the third day of creation became a carpenter's son and died on a tree to save you from your sins. Jesus took on flesh to fight your greatest battle. He knows your sorrows. He's acquainted with grief.[6] He was tempted in every way just like we are.[7] Yet he perfectly obeyed and fulfilled the law and never sinned. He is the answer to every

---

5. Isa 7:14; Matt 1:22–23.
6. Isaiah 53.
7. Heb 4:15.

PART THREE—JESUS THE SUFFERING SERVANT

promise God ever made.[8] From the creation of the world, to every covenant in the Old Testament, to the arms of a lowly carpenter descended from David, Jesus has and always will be the plan. The plan to save us from our sin. To give us freedom. To give us hope. To give us a new family legacy. So how do we gain acceptance into his family? There's no magic prayer to pray or credentials to earn your way to God. Jesus came preaching "Repent and believe,"[9] and following him is as simple as that. All you have to do is make a choice to turn from your sin, accept Jesus' sacrifice on the cross, and follow him.

I love how the *New Dictionary of Theology* concludes the entry about the incarnation. It is the perfect conclusion to this chapter as we have dwelled on the significance of God coming as a baby to fulfil the promises of God. Promises that are still being fulfilled for you today.

> To save us God came not in his full glory as God but rather as man; as a baby crying in his mother's arms, requiring feeding and changing, and as a condemned criminal on a cross. He hid his glory, he limited himself. Remaining one with and equal to God he took the form of a slave. By becoming one with us, he was able to share our sorrows, bear our burdens, atone for our sins and unite us to God.[10]

This should cause us to shout out loud along with the apostle Paul, "Thanks be to God through Jesus Christ our Lord!" For we have been given a new identity in Christ. A new lineage in his family. We are chosen and adopted as children of God. And because of that, we will never be the same.

---

8. 2 Cor 1:20.
9. Mark 1:15.
10. Letham, "Incarnation," 336.

Chapter Eleven

Living in the Already/Not Yet
The Battle of Redemption

Romans 8:22–25

²² For we know that the whole creation has been groaning together in the pains of childbirth until now. ²³ And not only the creation, but we ourselves, who have the firstfruits of the Spirit, groan inwardly as we wait eagerly for adoption as sons, the redemption of our bodies. ²⁴ For in this hope we were saved. Now hope that is seen is not hope. For who hopes for what he sees? ²⁵ But if we hope for what we do not see, we wait for it with patience.

REMEMBER JOSHUA'S STORY? HE trusted God to fulfill the promise he made to lead his people to a land flowing with milk and honey, but Joshua still had to fight. The land wasn't simply handed to him, even though God was helping them see the victory in each battle. It is the same with us in our battles. Like Adam and Eve, we have a choice. God wants you to have abundant life. Abundant life that is only found in him. Yet, there are battles and hardship and suffering amidst that Promised Land life. We have to act upon God's Word in obedience in order to see the victories he promises and not just expect him to hand it to us. You can be assured, though, that even in your battles, God is fighting for you.

This can be seen no more clearly than when the King of the cosmos came to the frontlines to fight our greatest and longest-lasting battle—sin. God took on human flesh, not to ride in as a conquering king like David and bring back the Promised Land, but to suffer and die to take the punishment we deserved. This battle is what has caused most of the evil and suffering in our life, whether directly through our sins or indirectly through others'. But Jesus' sacrifice on the cross and resurrection from the dead accomplished exactly what he sought to do—defeat sin and death. Yet evil and suffering still exist. Life is still hard. Tears are still real. The struggle of sin is still a constant battle.

So if we have been given victory in Jesus, why is the battle still waged? Why do we still struggle to overcome temptation? Why do we still fight with our children and our spouse? Why do we still toil to make ends meet? Why is so much of the world still impoverished? Why do people still die? Why are there still murders and thefts and bullying? Why is there still pain and heartbreak and depression and anxiety and doubts and fears? Why is so much of this world still so incredibly broken?

The Already and Not Yet

The reason we still face battles every day is because we live in the *already/ not yet*. Jesus has *already* defeated sin and Satan, but it is *not yet* fully realized. Jesus has crushed the head of that ancient serpent, yet he has not cast that beast into the lake of fire that burns forever and ever.[1] This can be illustrated in the difference between D-Day and V-Day. The battle at Normandy on June 6, 1944, also referred to as D-Day, essentially ended World War II. Yet the battles were not over after that invasion. People still died after Normandy. It wasn't until V-Day, or Victory in Europe day, on May 8, 1945 that the war was officially over, nearly a year after D-Day. Right now, we are living between D-Day and V-Day. The battle has been fought. The victory has been decided. But there are and will still be casualties until that victory is finally actualized.

Have you ever gone up behind someone to push them into a pool or lake, or have you ever been pushed in by someone else? What do you normally do as you are falling down? You flail your arms and try to grab

---

1. Rev 20:10.

at anything you can to drag the person who pushed you down with you. Satan knows he is a defeated foe. He knew that when he was first cast out of heaven thousands of years ago. The head of that serpent has been stomped on by Jesus, but he's still thrashing around on the floor trying to take down as many people as he can with him. This makes him all the more dangerous. He will lead many astray in the last days.[2] He promises abundant life just like Jesus does, only Satan's way leads to death. And many will follow it. But there is coming a day when Satan gets what he deserves. The victory that has been won on the cross will be finally and fully realized, and there will be no more fight. It is hope in that final victory that allows us to fight and live through the battles we face now. The hope of the *already* fuels our fighting in the *not yet*.

Although God came to dwell with his people in the person of Jesus, the fulfillment of all the promises have yet to be fully realized. He has crushed the head of the serpent. He has risen from the dead. He has ushered in his rule and reign and is the King of every person's heart who places their faith in him. Although his spiritual rule and reign has been realized, creation still groans. Romans 8:22–25 explains the *already/not yet* dichotomy that we live in so perfectly:

> [22] For we know that the whole creation has been groaning together in the pains of childbirth until now. [23] And not only the creation, but we ourselves, who have the firstfruits of the Spirit, groan inwardly as we wait eagerly for adoption as sons, the redemption of our bodies. [24] For in this hope we were saved. Now hope that is seen is not hope. For who hopes for what he sees? [25] But if we hope for what we do not see, we wait for it with patience.

This concept of the *already* but *not yet* was formulated by Gerhardus Vos, a theologian from Princeton, in the early 1900s. In the 1950s, George Eldon Ladd, a professor at Fuller Theological Seminary, further expanded on this idea by proposing that the kingdom of God has two meanings: (1) God's authority and right to rule, and (2) the realm in which God exercises his authority. According to Scripture, the kingdom is portrayed as both a realm that can be entered presently and one that will be entered in the future. Ladd concluded that the kingdom of God exists in both the present and the future.[3]

---

2. Matt 24:24.
3. Got Questions, "What is the concept of 'already not yet'?"

PART THREE—JESUS THE SUFFERING SERVANT

David Briones of Westminster Theological Seminary explains it like this:

> For now, Christians live in a great theological tension: we already possess every spiritual blessing in Christ, but we do not experience the fullness of these blessings yet. In one sense, we are already adopted, redeemed, sanctified, and saved; in another, these experiences are not yet fully ours. Underneath this theological and practical tension are the two comings of Christ. In his first coming, he inaugurated the last days; in his second coming, he will complete them. In the meantime, we live for now in "the overlap of the ages."[4]

Ladd further shows the reality of our *already, not-yet* through some biblical examples. We are:

- *already* adopted in Christ (Rom 8:15), but *not yet* adopted (Rom 8:23);
- *already* redeemed in Christ (Eph 1:7), but *not yet* redeemed (Eph 4:30);
- *already* sanctified in Christ (1 Cor 1:2), but *not yet* sanctified (1 Thess 5:23–24);
- *already* saved in Christ (Eph 2:8), but *not yet* saved (Rom 5:9);
- *already* raised with Christ (Eph 2:6), but *not yet* raised (1 Cor 15:52).

We exist in a theological paradox, where through our faith in Christ we possess spiritual blessings already, yet we do not fully experience the complete enjoyment of these blessings. This is the essence of a life of faith, where we hold onto the assurance of future hope and the conviction of present unseen realities.[5] It is a life lived in the tension between the times, navigating the balance between the already and the not yet.

Theology of Salvation

The first coming of Jesus was announced as "good news of great joy." What makes something good news though? Good news for one person could be bad news for another. "Good news! I got the promotion!" But it's bad news if you are the person who was passed over for the same job. The news of

---

4. Briones, "Already, Not Yet."
5. Heb 11:1.

the first coming of Jesus, though, was announced as good news "for all the people."⁶ This means that the content of what makes the news good must be available to all the people. So what makes the good news of Jesus good? The goodness of the news of the first coming of Jesus is that salvation, or redemption, is freely offered to all. The angel stated as much after he announced the good news. "For unto you is born this day in the city of David a Savior, who is Christ the Lord."⁷ This is the gospel, which literally means good news. Jesus came to bring salvation.

When studying the theology of salvation, it can be divided into three groupings or tenses: justification, sanctification, and glorification. These distinct groupings give further explanation to how Jesus has both *already* and *not yet* dealt with our sin as our Savior. Sin wreaks havoc on everything. Suffering exists because sin exists. And Jesus has *already* defeated sin, although it has *not yet* been fully realized, which matters for how we walk through our hardships now. I want to briefly explain each of these aspects of salvation, but more importantly, I want us to see how it affects our suffering *already*. Each one of these matters for why Jesus came, and each one of these is incredible, good news of great joy that is for all people. Yes, even you.

Justification

Imagine you committed a heinous crime. And there was a trail of crimes in the wake of your heinous crime that is longer than you can count on all your fingers and toes. After all, sin has a way of leading to more sin. After running from the authorities for months, you are finally captured. As you await your trial and sentencing, you know there is no way you will be acquitted. There's no use in even pleading not guilty. There's far too much evidence. As you approach the judge, you do so with your head down and shuffled feet. You know the words that are about to reverberate through your skull and haunt you for the rest of your days. As you anticipate the "Guilty!" verdict to resound, you think you misheard. What did the judge say? "*Not* guilty"? How can that be?

You come to find out that someone else took your punishment. Someone that was truly not guilty. They took the punishment that you deserved. That's what Jesus did for us, as we see from Gal 3:13–14:

6. Luke 2:10.
7. Luke 2:11.

PART THREE—JESUS THE SUFFERING SERVANT

¹³ Christ redeemed us from the curse of the law by becoming a curse for us—for it is written, "Cursed is everyone who is hanged on a tree"— ¹⁴ so that in Christ Jesus the blessing of Abraham might come to the Gentiles, so that we might receive the promised Spirit through faith.

That is what justification is. The moment you repent and believe in Jesus, God the Father says, "Not guilty," because Jesus has taken the punishment you deserved. It's the cosmic reality for each person who has placed their faith in him. The only way to live an abundant life is by giving Christ Jesus your whole heart of which he came to conquer.

Many of our hardships and suffering in life have come from the struggle against sin and its consequences. And while there are still consequences to sin even after we have given our lives to Jesus, there is now no condemnation[8] for sin because justification removes our guilt and shame. Being justified before the Judge of all the earth[9] ensures that our sins are forgiven. If we weren't justified, we would have consequences and condemnation, but Jesus bore all the weight of our guilt and shame and was crushed by the burden of our condemnation. That's a weight we no longer have to bear, even though we will forever struggle with sin in this *not-yet* world.

But what about suffering that does not come from our sin? How does justification help with that? The price that Jesus paid and the suffering that he endured, unites us with him when we suffer. He was prophesied as the "Suffering Servant."[10] He knows what it is to hurt, hunger, and mourn. He didn't have to pay that price because he is God and the perfect Judge.[11] But he willingly entered into our suffering. And he endured even through death itself. The last words that he spoke before he ascended into heaven were, "And behold, I am with you always, to the end of the age."[12] The one who suffered in our place is with us amidst our suffering, until there is no more suffering.

8. Rom 8:1.
9. Gen 18:25.
10. Isaiah 53.
11. 2 Tim 4:1.
12. Matt 28:20.

Sanctification

Though those who are in Christ are legally not guilty, we don't fully live out that reality yet. You and I both know that sin remains a constant battle every day. Christian perfectionism is not attainable as the apostle Paul alluded to in Romans 7 when he says, "For I delight in the law of God, in my inner being, but I see in my members another law waging war against the law of my mind making me captive to the law of sin that dwells in my members."[13] I'm sure you can relate to his struggle when he laments, "For I have the desire to do what is right, but not the ability to carry it out."[14] Though we are legally not guilty according to the judge of all the earth, our actions so often don't correspond with that reality. That's why Paul ultimately cries, "Wretched man that I am! Who will deliver me from this body of death? Thanks be to God through Jesus Christ our Lord!"[15]

Sanctification is a continual growing in Christlikeness. It follows our being justified by God. "In justification, God at the beginning of Christian life declares us acquitted. In sanctification, God accomplishes his will in us as Christian life proceeds."[16] Sanctification helps us in our suffering first because suffering is a means of sanctification. Suffering has a way of stripping away everything that doesn't truly matter. It produces Christlike characteristics in us that we would never have otherwise.[17] Much like with precious metals, the fiery furnace of hardship burns away impurities, resulting in the reflection of Christ being seen in what was once a cloudy and impure life. And second, sanctification helps us amidst our suffering because as we grow in Christlikeness, it's not just our life that looks different, but it's our faith. We grow in trust as we grow in Christ. So whatever trial we find ourselves in, we trust God amidst it, to either remove it or give us strength to persevere through it. And we trust that our hardships are for good purposes even if we don't understand what those purposes are.

---

13. Rom 7:22–23.
14. Rom 7:18.
15. Rom 7:24–25.
16. White, "Sanctification," 770–72.
17. Rom 5:3–5.

PART THREE—JESUS THE SUFFERING SERVANT

Glorification

Though the wages of sin is death,[18] there is coming a day when the battle with sin will be over. There is coming a day, soon on the horizon, when all will be made new. Jesus will reign in victory forever. And we will reign with him.[19] There will be a final battle to end all battles and a day when there will be no more death, because there will be no more sin, for the former things will have passed away.[20] Glorification is the *not yet* of our present salvation. And the certain future glorification is of utmost importance for how we persevere through our sufferings here and now. The last four chapters of this book are devoted to the final and forever reign of Christ over sin, suffering, and death itself, which will go more in depth into this *not-yet* glorification. But even now, there is still hope. Hope that helps you fight your battles as you look towards the day when there will be no more battles. Justification, sanctification, and glorification all point to Christ's redemptive work on the cross, which is the lens we should look through at our suffering as well.

No Redemption Without Suffering

Hope was born at Christmas when God came to dwell with his sinful creation in order to redeem his sinful creation. This baby named Jesus grew in wisdom and stature, in favor with God and man,[21] and when he was around thirty years old, he began teaching and preaching publicly about the kingdom of heaven. He performed miracles. He ate with sinners. He gave people living water they had never tasted before. He set an example on how to love and serve but he also confronted man's hypocrisy and called people out of their sin. He wasn't just their savior but also their teacher, doctor and friend. He was the one they had been waiting for. The one the prophets foretold about. He was their hope. But all seemed lost when God allowed him to suffer the worst imaginable death possible.

Do you know Jesus could have come at any time in history to save his people from their sins, but the Father destined him to come during Roman rule, when crucifixion was a common practice? Any other type of

18. Rom 3:23.
19. 2 Tim 2:12.
20. Rev 21:4.
21. Luke 2:52.

death seems trivial in comparison to this one. In the garden of Gethsemane the night before he was killed, Jesus prayed that God would let this cup of suffering pass from him. He was so distraught thinking about it, he was sweating drops of blood. He knew it was going to be painful, excruciating—just like the word crucifixion stems from. And taking the punishment we deserved would transpose all our sin on him, separating him for the first time from God the Father whom he had been one with forever. Still, Jesus submitted to the Father's will.

Often we pray that God would allow the cup of suffering to pass from us. Or if we are already in the midst of suffering we pray it doesn't last long. Elisabeth Elliot has known much suffering in her life, starting with her first husband being martyred by the Auca Indians whom he was trying to reach with the gospel and then her second husband dying of cancer. But she learned through her suffering to submit her will to God. In her book, *Suffering is Never for Nothing*, she states:

> Whatever is in the cup that God is offering to me, whether it be pain and sorrow and suffering and grief along with the many more joys, I'm willing to take it because I trust Him. Because I know that what God wants for me is the very best. I will receive this thing in His name.
>
> I need pain sometimes because God has something bigger in mind. It is never for nothing. And so I say Lord, in Jesus' name, by Your grace I accept it.[22]

Jesus accepted the cup the Father had for him because he was working something greater than his pain in that moment. The Father could have spared him, but then we would have no redemption from our sins. And as Elliot goes on to say, "There is, in fact, no redemptive work done anywhere without suffering."[23] The Father allowed his son to bear the punishment we deserved because that was the greatest way he could show his love and display his glory to the world. Through the cross and empty tomb, Jesus defeated our ancient enemy, sin and death. We must live with a greater sense of the gravity of sin and the grandeur of God in order to truly appreciate the gospel by which we have been saved.

Until Jesus comes back, we will continue to battle our flesh because it is part of who we are and part of living in a broken, sinful world. It's a suffering we must not give up battling though. Through Jesus's sacrifice on

22. Elliot, *Suffering Is Never for Nothing*, 54.
23. Elliot, *Suffering is Never for Nothing*, 104.

the cross, we see how God is glorified through suffering. How redemption is made possible through suffering. And how our everyday sufferings can point to the love and hope of Jesus. Because there is always a greater purpose to suffering. Without it, we would not have justification, sanctification and glorification. All suffering and redemption can be looked at through this three-part lens. So when we think our suffering will overtake us and all hope is lost, may we remember along with Elliot:

> That old, rugged cross so despised by the world. The very worst thing that ever happened in human history turns out to be the very best thing because it saved me. It saves the world. And so God's love, which was represented, demonstrated to us in His giving His Son Jesus to die on the cross, has been brought together in harmony with suffering.[24]

---

24. Elliot, *Suffering is Never for Nothing*, 13.

Chapter Twelve

Trusting in the Empty Tomb
The Battle of Living Again

---

1 Peter 1:3–9

³ Blessed be the God and Father of our Lord Jesus Christ! According to his great mercy, he has caused us to be born again to a living hope through the resurrection of Jesus Christ from the dead, ⁴ to an inheritance that is imperishable, undefiled, and unfading, kept in heaven for you, ⁵ who by God's power are being guarded through faith for a salvation ready to be revealed in the last time. ⁶ In this you rejoice, though now for a little while, if necessary, you have been grieved by various trials, ⁷ so that the tested genuineness of your faith—more precious than gold that perishes though it is tested by fire—may be found to result in praise and glory and honor at the revelation of Jesus Christ. ⁸ Though you have not seen him, you love him. Though you do not now see him, you believe in him and rejoice with joy that is inexpressible and filled with glory, ⁹ obtaining the outcome of your faith, the salvation of your souls.

DEATH. IT'S A COLD, hard, ever-too-close reality. Death of some sort is likely what has led you to read this book. The death of a loved one, the death of a

PART THREE—JESUS THE SUFFERING SERVANT

dream, the death of a way of life, the death of your past, the death of missed opportunities, the death of your planned future due to past mistakes, the death of the expectation you had for how your life would turn out when you are now facing a reality that is drastically different. Or it's the small, less noticeable moments we die inside when we doubt God and ourselves, live in fear, or compare ourselves to those we can never measure up to. Death doesn't just come from dying, but it arises in a million different ways from living in a broken and sinful world.

From the beginning, original sin has brought about the perpetual dying of all creation, for "The wages of sin is death."[1] And all creation, of which you and I are a part, has been groaning and hoping and crying out for a great reversal ever since. We long for an end to the suffering, heartache, pain, uncertainty, fear and feelings that things just aren't quite right.

Hebrews 9:27 tells us, "It is appointed for man to die once. . ." but Christians realize that the story does not end. Not that the story does not end *there*. The story does not *end* . . . at all . . . because there are no mortal people. Hebrews 9:27 continues, "It is appointed for man to die once, and after that comes judgment," meaning, there is life beyond death. It is not the end. And there is life not just after physical death but in this life as well. There can be life after the death of your dream. There can be life after the loss of your perceived future. There can be life after the heartache, doubts, and fears that come from all sorts of a million little deaths we face every day and the ones that loom largest over us, too. There is life after death. There is resurrection because of the resurrection of Jesus, and it doesn't just affect your forever. It affects your *now*.

N.T. Wright says, "Though the literal 'resurrection' of which the early Christians spoke remained firmly in the future, it coloured and gave shape to present Christian living as well."[2] Francis Schaeffer explains the same concept like this: "The reality of the resurrection is not something to push off into a strange dimension. It is meaningful in our normal dimension."[3] The resurrection of Jesus gives us hope here and now.

Hope is found in a person and an event. The person is Jesus. The event is the resurrection. The death of Jesus was the fatal blow to the enemy, but his resurrection was the victory. And the result of Jesus being alive is abundance of life for all who believe and follow him. Without the resurrection,

---

1. Rom 6:23.
2. Wright, *Resurrection of the Son of God*, 210.
3. Schaeffer, *True Spirituality*, 29.

there would be no hope. But because of the resurrection, the reality in which you are suffering is one in which Jesus is already risen, meaning that life can always spring from death. And in that, there is always hope. Yet in order to be able to apply the reality of this hope to our present lives, we must first see the reality of the resurrection. Due to the nature of the evidence, let me step aside for a moment and allow you to hear from top experts on this highly debated subject.

The Reality of Christ's Resurrection

One of the leading scholars regarding the historicity of the resurrection of Jesus is a distinguished research professor of apologetics and philosophy from Liberty University, Gary Habermas. One of his former students, Michael Licona (who is an expert on the topic as well) in his own scholarly work on the resurrection noted:

> At present Habermas has an unpublished bibliography of academic literature written on the subject of Jesus' resurrection from 1975 to the present in German, French and English. He has told me that there are in the neighborhood of 3,400 sources. He has cataloged the positions of scholars on more than one hundred topics directly related to the resurrection of Jesus in a roughly formatted Microsoft Word document more than six hundred pages in length.[4]

All that to say Habermas is well read and knows the arguments on both sides of the spectrum relating to Jesus' resurrection. There are five "minimal facts" or bedrocks that Habermas and Licona[5] state as historical realities of the resurrection, meaning it is historically certain that they happened because of the evidence that backs it up:

(i) Jesus' death by crucifixion,

(ii) his disciples' belief that he appeared to them,

(iii) Paul's conversion,

(iv) James' conversion, and

(v) the empty tomb.

---

4. Licona, *Resurrection of Jesus*, 278.
5. Licona, *Resurrection of Jesus*, 75.

PART THREE—JESUS THE SUFFERING SERVANT

What we're going to do in this chapter is walk through these five historical realities. (I realize the tone of this chapter is a little different and the content is a little more academic, but please press on. This information matters!) Here's what we see first: it is historical fact that Jesus died by crucifixion. Even Bart Ehrman, one of the world's leading critics of the New Testament states, "One of the most certain facts of history is that Jesus was crucified on orders of the Roman prefect of Judea, Pontius Pilate."[6] This is important as we look at the resurrection, because you can't rise from the dead if you never died.

Some religions and persuasions claim that a look-alike or imposter took the place of Jesus on the cross, and Jesus himself never died. Or they believe that God took him before he died. Another theory is that Jesus was near to the point of death when they took him off the cross but then recovered. In history, there is only one documented survival of a crucifixion victim, which was recorded by the Jewish historian Josephus. And in that case the person was taken down early under special circumstances and still barely survived, while two others did not survive. Hear his own recounting of it:

> And when I was sent by Titus Caesar with Cerealins, and a thousand horsemen, to a certain village called Thecoa, in order to know whether it were a place fit for a camp, as I came back, I saw many captives crucified, and remembered three of them as my former acquaintance. I was very sorry at this in my mind, and went with tears in my eyes to Titus, and told him of them; so he immediately commanded them to be taken down, and to have the greatest care taken of them, in order to their recovery; yet two of them died under the physician's hands, while the third recovered.[7]

If Jesus did happen to survive crucifixion—which is far-fetched and lacking evidence, given the fact that on top of being crucified, Jesus was also pierced in the side with a spear before being taken down—his disciples would not have worshiped him as God but would rather have tried to help mend his wounds, like these in Josephus' account did. But that's not how they approached him. They approached him as gloriously resurrected.

Second, it is historical fact that Jesus' disciples *believed* he appeared to them, risen from the dead. But what would it take for him to have actually appeared to them? Some have proposed the disciples were hallucinating,

---

6. Ehrman, *New Testament*, 261–62.
7. Josephus, *Life of Flavius Josephus*, 76.

that they thought they saw Jesus but didn't really. There have been many cases of people being so grieved by the death of a loved one that they thought they saw them, which could have been the case if it was an isolated incident, maybe. But that's not how it happened. Jesus appeared to different people, at different times, in different places over a forty-day period. He even had meals with people and was physically touched by them, ensuring that he wasn't a ghost or hallucination.

Hear from the earliest source we have in our New Testament from 1 Cor 15:1–8, written by the apostle Paul. It is an oral testimony that was passed down between believers starting within months or years of the resurrection event.

> ¹Now I would remind you, brothers, of the gospel I preached to you, which you received, in which you stand, ²and by which you are being saved, if you hold fast to the word I preached to you—unless you believed in vain. ³For I delivered to you as of first importance what I also received: that Christ died for our sins in accordance with the Scriptures, ⁴that he was buried, that he was raised on the third day in accordance with the Scriptures, ⁵and that he appeared to Cephas, then to the twelve. ⁶Then he appeared to more than five hundred brothers at one time, most of whom are still alive, though some have fallen asleep. ⁷Then he appeared to James, then to all the apostles. ⁸Last of all, as to one untimely born, he appeared also to me.

Just like people don't have shared dreams at night, people don't have shared hallucinations over a period of time among different people in different places. In the case of Jesus, he appeared to over five hundred people over a forty day period.

Third, historical bedrocks number (iii) and (iv) have to do with the conversion of two people, Paul and James. We just read Paul's account. He talks about himself as one "untimely born." He goes on in verses 9 and 10 to say, "For I am the least of the apostles, unworthy to be called an apostle, because I persecuted the church of God. But by the grace of God I am what I am..." Paul was converted from being a persecutor of Christians to being the chief missionary for Christianity. And the sole reason for his drastic conversion was because he saw Jesus alive.

The James in reference to number (iv) is one of the brothers of Jesus. It's true that your family typically knows you the best. But for James, who grew up with Jesus and knew him more than most other people, he didn't believe that Jesus was the Messiah before Jesus' death and crucifixion.[8] Much like you wouldn't want to give your older brother credit for being a pro baseball player just because he's good at baseball. Unless he actually does make it to the pros. So what was the turning point for James? Seeing Jesus *after* the resurrection sealed the deal that Jesus was truly the Messiah he had been claiming. That fact is so important that it was included in this early oral testimony about the resurrection that was circulated.[9] Not only did James become a follower of Jesus, but he became the leader of the church in Jerusalem.

Both of these men came to faith, of which is a historical reality, precisely because they believed Jesus rose from the dead. And they believed because they saw him resurrected. Not only did these once disbelievers believe in him, but they lived and died for him, too. James was stoned to death for his belief in Jesus in AD 62, and Paul had his head cut off for his belief in Jesus in AD 68. Both gave their life for what they knew to be true. Jesus had risen from the dead.

This leads us to the final historical fact, the empty tomb. If Jesus' tomb wasn't empty, why did the Roman authorities not parade the body of Jesus around town to dispel their claims? Everyone was saying he was raised from the dead. All they would have to say is, *"No he's not. Look!"* and show the body. Instead, they made up a lie as to why the tomb was empty, which actually affirms the historicity that the tomb was really empty. They said his disciples stole the body.[10] Ancient extra-biblical sources confirm this, too. Hear Gary Habermas again:

> Before answering the issue concerning Jesus' resurrection, we will initially address the. . .point of whether the empty tomb can be established as historical by this extra biblical evidence alone. There are some strong considerations in its favor. First, the Jewish sources which we have examined admit the empty tomb, thereby providing evidence from hostile documents. Josephus notes the disciples' belief in Jesus' resurrection, while the Toledoth Jesu specifically acknowledges the empty tomb. Justin Martyr and Tertullian confirm Matt. 28:11–15 by asserting that Jewish leaders were still admitting the empty tomb over a century later. While these Jewish sources (with the exception of Josephus) teach that the body was stolen or moved, they still admit the empty tomb.

8. John 7:5.
9. 1 Cor 15:7.
10. Matt 28:13.

Second, there are apparently no ancient sources which assert that the tomb still contained Jesus' body. While such an argument from silence does not prove anything, it is made stronger by the first consideration from the hostile sources and further complements it. Third, our study has shown that Jesus taught in Palestine and was crucified and buried in Jerusalem under Pontius Pilate. These sources assert that Christianity had its beginnings in the same location. But could Christianity have survived in this location, based on its central claim that Jesus was raised from the dead, if the tomb had not been empty? It must be remembered that the resurrection of the body was the predominant view of first century Jews. To declare a bodily resurrection if the body was still in a nearby tomb points out the dilemma here. Of all places. evidence was readily available in Jerusalem to disprove this central tenet of Christian belief. The Jewish leaders had both a motive and the means to get such evidence if it were available. As expressed by historian of antiquity, Paul Maier, speaking of the birth of Christianity: "But this is the very last place it could have started if Jesus' tomb had remained occupied, since anyone producing a dead Jesus would have driven a wooden stake through the heart of an incipient Christianity inflamed by his supposed resurrection.[11]

So the predominant view after Jesus's body was missing was that the disciples stole the body. It's even recorded in Scripture as a claim the Jewish leaders held. The disciples could not have stolen the body though, because they neither had motive nor the ability. These fishermen and tax collectors would have had to turn into essentially trained ninjas to overcome powerful Roman guards and get the body of Jesus from them. They didn't have the ability. Nor did they have the motive. Every single one of his followers died for their belief in Jesus and his resurrection. Not a single one said, *"Nope. We took him. It's all a hoax."* They were stoned to death, decapitated, crucified upside down, banished, and more.

Chuck Colson, who was sentenced to jail time as part of President Nixon's Watergate scandal and became a devoted Christian around that same time, says about the disciples' lack of motive:

> Can anyone believe that for fifty years that Jesus' disciples were willing to be ostracized, beaten, persecuted, and all but one of them suffer a martyr's death–without ever renouncing their conviction that they had seen Jesus bodily resurrected? Does anyone really think the disciples could have maintained a lie all that time under

---

11. Habermas, "Ancient Non-Christian Sources."

PART THREE—JESUS THE SUFFERING SERVANT

that kind of pressure? No, someone would have cracked, just as we did so easily in Watergate. Someone would have acted as John Dean did and turned state's evidence. There would have been some kind of smoking gun, or a deathbed confession. So why didn't they crack? Because they had come face to face with the living God. They could not deny what they had seen. The fact is that people will give their lives for what they believe is true, but they will never give their lives for what they know is a lie. The Watergate cover-up proves that 12 powerful men in modern America couldn't keep a lie–and that 12 powerless men 2,000 years ago couldn't have been telling anything but the truth.[12]

There is so much more we could say about all of this. It's one thing to deny the realities of the resurrection of Jesus. It's another thing to provide evidence for the denials. As we have seen through these five major arguments, there is a severe lack of evidence for every contrary theory to the resurrection of Jesus. It is a continual grasping at straws in order to deny what one doesn't want to believe. Jesus really rose. And that really matters. It matters more than anything. Not just for each person's eternity, for salvation is only by and because of Jesus' death and resurrection, but it matters for each person's *now*.

Present Hope

So if we believe the evidence that points to the fact that Jesus indeed rose from the grave, how does that help us in our present suffering? After all, that's why you're reading this book, right? You need hope. Hope is found in the living, breathing Jesus. Schaeffer beautifully takes us from the historicity of the resurrection to its application in our everyday life:

> The glory and wonder of Christ are not pushed off into a world that is "other" than our own . . . There is a real, historic death of Jesus Christ. There is a real, historic Resurrection. And there is a real, historic future glorification that is meaningful in terms of space, time, and history: *our own* space, time, and history. The Bible says that the day will come when both saved and unsaved men will look upon the glorified Christ. They will see him. Every man will see him, not as a religious idea, but glorified, in a real space-time situation. . .but not only will he be so, but that he is so *now*.[13]

12. https://www.breakpoint.org/watergate-and-the-resurrection/
13. Schaeffer, *True Spirituality*, 33.

TRUSTING IN THE EMPTY TOMB

I pray that you will be able to take hold of that reality for yourself and your present situation. In N.T. Wright's scholarly work on the resurrection, he states, "The hope of resurrection, here as elsewhere, is invoked to sustain those who are undergoing persecution."[14] And even though you might not be facing persecution like the early believers, the reality of the resurrection can fuel you to persevere through anything you face, just like it did for them. You might be thinking, "But they *saw* him. It was more real for them." It's easy to let thoughts like that keep you from applying the hope of the resurrection to your current life and situation. But Jesus said, "Blessed are those who have not seen and yet have believed."[15] And here's the deal, if Jesus really rose for them, he is really risen for you, too. Not just *then*, but in our present lives *now*.

Schaeffer explains this reality and its implications better than anyone. In reference to Rom 6:4, which states "We were buried therefore with him by baptism into death, in order that, just as Christ was raised from the dead by the glory of the Father, we too might walk in newness of life." Schaeffer says:

> When? Right Now! This is the basic consideration of the Christian life. First, Christ died in history. Second, Christ rose in history. Third, we died with Christ in history, when we accepted him as our Savior. Fourth, we will be raised in history, when he comes again. Fifth, we are to live by faith now as though we were now dead, already have died. And sixth, we are to live now by faith as though we have now already been raised from the dead.
>
> Now what does this mean in practice, so that it will not be just words going over our heads? First of all, it certainly means this: that in our thoughts and lives now we are to live *as though we had already died, been to heaven, and come back again as risen.*[16]

Even though this world tends towards death, God is making all things new. Jesus spoke about it when he said:

> [1] Let not your hearts be troubled. Believe in God; believe also in me. [2] In my Father's house are many rooms. If it were not so, would I have told you that I go to prepare a place for you? [3] And if I go

---

14. Wright, *Resurrection*, 498.
15. John 20:29.
16. Schaeffer, *True Spirituality*, 37.

and prepare a place for you, I will come again and will take you to myself, that where I am you may be also.[17]

Let the excitement and joys of that future, forever home fill every moment of this broken life on this broken earth for you. C. S. Lewis beautifully shows this grand reversal and renewal that the living Jesus brings and the implications of what he is currently doing when he says, "We live amid all the anomalies, inconveniences, hopes, and excitements of a house that is being rebuilt."[18]

What is your house being rebuilt with? Is it the bitterness of your suffering that has left you empty, discouraged, angry, or callused? Or is it the joy of your suffering that has left you hopeful, trusting, full of grace, and confident in God's love and faithfulness? The thing about hope is it doesn't remove us from our hardships. But it is *the* factor that allows us to persevere through our hardships. Hope doesn't just make life bearable. It provides joy, meaning, and purpose amidst the pain. What an incredible and beautiful reversal. Death to life. Not just with Christ's resurrection. But for us and within us.

Hear me. There *is* hope. Jesus *is* alive. Even now. And as he is alive, even amidst the hardships and inconveniences and death, let that reality fill you with hope and excitement, because if you are in him, one day you will be with him. Just as the disciples were able to endure all hardships because they had seen firsthand the resurrected Jesus, we are able to live in light of the resurrection now, certain of the hope that we cling to. And that matters. Even and especially today.

So whatever you're going through, there is hope. Jesus is alive. This darkness won't last forever because the Son is risen. He is risen indeed.

---

17. John 14:1–3.
18. Lewis, *Miracles*, 155.

PART FOUR

JESUS THE CONQUERING KING
The Final End of Suffering and Hope

Chapter Thirteen

Fighting a Kingdom You Cannot See
The Battle of Spiritual Warfare

Ephesians 6:12–13

¹² For we do not wrestle against flesh and blood, but against the rulers, against the authorities, against the cosmic powers over this present darkness, against the spiritual forces of evil in the heavenly places. ¹³ Therefore take up the whole armor of God, that you may be able to withstand in the evil day, and having done all, to stand firm.

THIS BOOK HAS BEEN all about battles. Battles in the Promised Land. Battles in life, especially the abundant Christian life where there is suffering, hardship, pain, loss, tears, striving, depression, and fear. This book has been about how to wade through those battles. How to trust God amidst them. How to cry out to the Helper. How to be redeemed. How to rest in his victory. And ultimately, how to still have hope, which is what this final section will focus on most.

We can have hope for our present battles because we know there is a final battle coming. A battle to end all battles. The book of Revelation talks about it and even though we can't unpack all of it in this book, we will touch on some highlights. Talk of "End Times" usually generates one of two responses: (1) It gives people the heebie-jeebies, and they don't want to think about it so they go on living as if it's never going to happen, or (2) people can't get enough of talking about it and want to pull out charts and graphs and study everything there is in order to be the most prepared. I fall somewhere in the middle of the two.

Just as there were numerous prophecies of the first coming of Jesus, there are many prophecies of his second coming. The first advent was prophesied that he would come lowly as a baby. The second advent prophesies that he will come mightily on a horse with a sword. And as surely as he came the first time, we can be sure he is coming again. But just as the people in Jesus' time had studied the prophecies regarding the coming Messiah, and many still missed him, why do we think we could have his second coming all figured out? We are no better than them.

There are some things we can know for sure about the end times, but there are also many details that we won't exactly understand until it arrives. So I'm going to major on the majors and minor on the minors. The final battle in Revelation seems a little strange to us, and some things we can only imagine from the vantage point of our limited worldview. But keep in mind, this battle does not begin and end all in one day. It's a battle that started in a garden, ends in a city, and in between are thousands of years of little battles between the kingdom of light and the kingdom of darkness, finding its culmination in the celebratory return of Christ. This final battle, known by many as the battle of Armageddon, presents Jesus in the Promised Land, bringing the final blow to that ancient serpent that has deceived the nations for far too long. And after this final battle, every striving and struggling and suffering and mourning will end. But before we get to the details of this final battle and celebrate its victory, I think it would benefit us to take a look at the nature of spiritual warfare that is raging right now between these two kingdoms. Because whether you realize it or not, you are already on one side or the other.

Satan's Kingdom Battle

Even though we don't know every detail for how the spiritual realm was created, like we do earth's creation in Genesis 1, we get some glimpses of it throughout Scripture. Just as we know Jesus came to bring about a kingdom under the authority of God, the kingdom of light, so we know there is another kingdom under the authority of Satan, the kingdom of darkness. But Satan wasn't always a part of the kingdom of darkness. Long before the creation of the world, Satan was in heaven with all the other angels, but his own pride caused his fall, and the earth became his dominion. There are two passages of the Bible that talk about this: (1) Ezek 28:12–17:

> [12] You were the signet of perfection,
>   full of wisdom and perfect in beauty.
> [13] You were in Eden, the garden of God;
>   every precious stone was your covering,
> sardius, topaz, and diamond,
>   beryl, onyx, and jasper,
> sapphire, emerald, and carbuncle;
>   and crafted in gold were your settings
>   and your engravings.
> On the day that you were created
>   they were prepared.
> [14] You were an anointed guardian cherub.
>   I placed you; you were on the holy mountain of God;
>   in the midst of the stones of fire you walked.
> [15] You were blameless in your ways
>   from the day you were created,
>   till unrighteousness was found in you.
> [16] In the abundance of your trade
>   you were filled with violence in your midst, and you sinned;
> so I cast you as a profane thing from the mountain of God,
>   and I destroyed you, O guardian cherub,
>   from the midst of the stones of fire.
> [17] Your heart was proud because of your beauty;
>   you corrupted your wisdom for the sake of your splendor.
> I cast you to the ground;
>   I exposed you before kings,
>   to feast their eyes on you.

And (2) Isa 14:12–17:

> [12] How you are fallen from heaven,
>   O Day Star, son of Dawn!
> How you are cut down to the ground,
>   you who laid the nations low!
> [13] You said in your heart,
>   "I will ascend to heaven;
> above the stars of God
>   I will set my throne on high;

> I will sit on the mount of assembly
>   in the far reaches of the north;
> ¹⁴ I will ascend above the heights of the clouds;
>   I will make myself like the Most High."
> ¹⁵ But you are brought down to Sheol,
>   to the far reaches of the pit.
> ¹⁶ Those who see you will stare at you
>   and ponder over you:
> "Is this the man who made the earth tremble,
>   who shook kingdoms,
> ¹⁷ who made the world like a desert
>   and overthrew its cities,
>   who did not let his prisoners go home?"

Something that's important to note about biblical prophecies, is that often times there are multiple meanings, subjects, and timelines all within the same prophecy. Take the Ezekiel passage for example, the author is talking about how Satan fell as well as addressing the King of Tyre in the same passage. Many biblical prophecies point to future *and* current timelines, physical *and* spiritual beings, and local *and* far-off realities, which means prophecies can have multiple meanings and interpretations. That is why reading Scripture as a whole is so important in order to get the full picture of its context.

After Satan fell, we see the first battle he waged against God in Genesis 3. That's where it all began for us. It was a battle for preserving Eden as kind of a proto-Promised Land, yet it was lost (or so it seemed), but not forever. And every story throughout the whole Old Testament since echoed a longing for the restoration of that initial land. From there Satan was given dominion over the earth, and as we learn in Job 1:6–7, he wanders to and fro on it, "prowl[ing] around like a roaring lion, seeking someone to devour."[1]

God's Kingdom Battles

After Adam and Eve sinned in the garden, the whole Old Testament proceeds to tell a story about the way God does two things: (1) God fights for his people in their faithful obedience. (2) He fights against his people in their sinful rebellion. Take Joshua for example. God fought for his people at Jericho and gave them the victory. But right after that at the battle of Ai,

---

1. 1 Pet 5:8.

they lose. Do you remember why? Because there was sin in the camp from disobedience to God in withholding some of the spoils of victory. So we see right there, back-to-back, an example of God fighting for his people and God fighting against his people. The same pattern is presented throughout the entire Old Testament narrative.

As the Old Testament advances, there is a narrowing of the line to David and his offspring. The Israelites keep wondering, "Where is the king that is going to come and restore our kingdom?" They know the promise, but it has yet been unfulfilled. And unfaithful king after unfaithful king comes, leading to an exile out of the Promised Land as a pointed judgment from God because of their rebellion. But years later, especially as they come back into the land around the time of the exilic prophets of Isaiah and Ezekiel, there's this echo of "He's coming! One day God's going to see fit to deliver us from all of this."

And that's exactly what you see happen when Jesus, the promised Messiah, comes. He comes as a new and better Adam. As a true Israel. And in every place where Israel failed to faithfully fight the battles that God had laid out before, Jesus succeeds. Ultimately Jesus' sacrifice on the cross demonstrates his active participation in spiritual warfare. The cross is the convergence of God fighting for his faithful people and fighting against his unfaithful people. Simultaneously Jesus is the true and faithful one God fights for, giving victory over Satan, sin, and death. But at the same time Jesus became like the unfaithful one when he took on our sins as a substitute. He faced judgment in the same way God repeatedly called his people to destroy their enemies in the Old Testament: wipe them out and show no mercy. That's what happens at the cross with Jesus in our place. It's a convergence of a long history of spiritual warfare. And thanks to Jesus, God is no longer fighting against those who are in Christ and have been reconciled to him by his blood.

Not only was Jesus's death on the cross the convergence of a battle against God's kingdom, but also his first coming was an active attack against Satan's kingdom. Because we are born sinners into this world that is under Satan's reign, we are automatically on his side and under his authority until we are redeemed by grace through faith in Christ. Each one of us were already on our way to hell, but the Father intervened and sent Jesus to pluck us from the fire. To rescue us. And we know who ultimately wins. It has been prophesied and promised, and God always keeps his promises. Satan and his followers know who wins, too. We see that played out in Jesus's ministry when he cast out demons, performed miracles, warded off Satan while being tempted in the wilderness, and rose from the empty tomb. Every one of these instances is a sign symbolizing the coming destruction of the demonic realm, which will ultimately be defeated in the final battle. But what does Jesus teach us about the spiritual warfare being waged right now? For we know Satan is not just waiting until the Battle of Armageddon to take up his sword. He has been fighting to take as many down with him since the creation of the world. And for those who are already redeemed, he is trying to steal as much abundant life from us as possible.

One of Jesus's most familiar teachings that is often overlooked in regards to spiritual warfare is the parable of the sower and the seeds.[2] In the parable, some seed falls on rocky soil, some falls on thorny soil, some falls on hard soil, and some falls on fertile soil. The seed represents the gospel. The soil represents our hearts. The seed that falls on the hard soil and is plucked up by the birds represents Satan snatching up the Truth before it takes root in our hearts. Then there is the seed that falls on rocky soil, and when the sun comes out, it withers, representing the persecution, anxieties and distractions of this world. And then there is the seed that falls among the thorns and is choked out, which represents the sinful desires of our flesh.

Through this parable, Jesus presents three hindrances to the gospel taking root in people's hearts: the devil, the world, and the flesh. Sometimes we give the enemy too much credit for having a hand in everything that goes wrong in our lives, when two thirds of the time it might be just part of living in a broken world or the result of our own sinful nature. But sometimes we don't consider the spiritual realm enough when there are forces at play for our attention and allegiance. Spiritual warfare is real, and we have to be on guard at all times. In this parable, only one out of the four seeds lands in good, fertile soil and takes root. If this was a literal representation of the odds of someone getting to heaven, it would be one in four. That's not very good. Thankfully, Jesus intervened on our behalf to help us beat those odds, and joining his team is an open invitation to all. If you haven't already, I pray you place your faith in Jesus. Say yes to the Holy Spirit who is drawing you to him, and open the door to receive eternal life.

---

2. Matthew 13.

Spiritual Armor for Battle

We know even after we join the right team, we are still going to have to battle the enemy who is trying to tempt us to sin, doubt God, and keep us from living the abundant Christian life. Now, the enemy can never take your redemption in Christ from you, so you can rest assured that you are secure in that,[3] but for everything else, how do we combat the kingdom of darkness? How do we protect and defend our Promised Land? Well the armor of God in Ephesians 6 is perhaps the most practical and instructive passage regarding individual yet corporate spiritual warfare:

> [10] Finally, be strong in the Lord and in the strength of his might. [11] Put on the whole armor of God, that you may be able to stand against the schemes of the devil. [12] For we do not wrestle against flesh and blood, but against the rulers, against the authorities, against the cosmic powers over this present darkness, against the spiritual forces of evil in the heavenly places. [13] Therefore take up the whole armor of God, that you may be able to withstand in the evil day, and having done all, to stand firm. [14] Stand therefore, having fastened on the belt of truth, and having put on the breastplate of righteousness, [15] and, as shoes for your feet, having put on the readiness given by the gospel of peace. [16] In all circumstances take up the shield of faith, with which you can extinguish all the flaming darts of the evil one; [17] and take the helmet of salvation, and the sword of the Spirit, which is the word of God, [18] praying at all times in the Spirit, with all prayer and supplication. To that end, keep alert with all perseverance, making supplication for all the saints, [19] and also for me, that words may be given to me in opening my mouth boldly to proclaim the mystery of the gospel, [20] for which I am an ambassador in chains, that I may declare it boldly, as I ought to speak.[4]

Most people just want to jump to the armor of God portion and how to apply each piece of the armor to our lives, but it's important to keep in mind that those who would have read this letter for the first time when Paul wrote it, would have recognized it to be first a corporate instruction, then an individual instruction. They would have been reading it aloud together as the church in Ephesus.

---

3. John 6:37.
4. Eph 6:10–20.

If you look at the original language, many parts of Paul's letter are written in plural. "Finally, be strong in the Lord," seems like a culminating aspect of a letter that has been written to an entire body of believers. And even some of the individual concepts, such as taking up the shield of faith, can have a corporate meaning. Looking at the historical context of shields in that era, they used them to line up side by side among many soldiers, creating a stronger barrier of protection as they marched towards an enemy together. We don't just fight battles on an individual basis as believers in Christ. All members of his body are fighting together against the kingdom of darkness.

Before Paul even gets to the armor of God part, he says to "be strong in the Lord and in the strength of his might." This is a both-and concept to spiritual warfare, not an either-or one. "Be strong in the Lord" means looking to God, not ourselves, and resting in his strength. But it's not saying, "God's got this. Just let him work in your life, while you sit back and do nothing." God does have it, but we can't stop there. We have to put forth effort when God is calling us to step out and fight. And we fight "in the strength of his might," which means that it is not by our own strength that we will overcome these battles and temptations. It's not by toughening up or having more will power that we will win. No, it is a supernatural strength that comes from the Lord and our identity in Christ that helps us to fight and overcome any battle we face.

Ephesians 6 provides us a solid foundation for grounding the battles we face in light of our identity in Christ. We are united with Jesus by faith. He is our helmet of salvation. He is our sword of the Spirit. He is the Truth. He is our breastplate of righteousness. Because he, the righteous one, is the one who earned salvation. He is the one that carried with him the gospel of peace. These are first true of Jesus, and only as a result of that, can they be true for those who are in him.

Throughout Paul's letters, there is a common theme of putting off the old man and putting on the new man, who is Christ.[5] He says to put off the old self and take up the new self, your new identity in Christ. And it seems like in Ephesians 6, Paul uses that same theme but comes at it from a different angle. When Paul says, "put on the armor of God," it is as if Paul is saying we should put on Christ, who is the armor of God. Christ is the only way we can defend ourselves against the enemy.

---

5. Eph 4:17–24.

Did you realize that all the pieces in the armor of God are meant to protect and defend, except for one? There is only one offensive weapon mentioned. In thinking of team sports, you can only be on the defense for so long before you must make a move to offense or else you will never win the game. The only offensive weapon we have in our battle against the kingdom of darkness is the sword of the spirit, which is the Word of God (the Bible). We can try to ward off Satan all day long with our best tactics, but unless we are in God's Word and memorizing Truth, we will never beat him. And since Satan knows Scripture too, as we see from him tempting Jesus in the wilderness, we must step up our game all the more. Because one of the best ways Satan trips us up is by twisting God's Word and getting us to believe something he didn't really say is true, like he did with Eve in the Garden of Eden, when Satan said to her, "Did God actually say. . .?"[6] So the Word of God is essential to not giving into Satan's battle scheme.

Keeping a Kingdom-Minded Perspective

Many times when talking of spiritual warfare, we are tempted to focus only on the battles that are going on within our own souls, such as lust, anxiety, disappointment, discouragement, despair, grief, or whatever else it may be. Then if we have time, we think of external battles we face, like persecution of the church, cultural influences, trials of this world, material woes, etc. Then last, if we even think of it at all, we might reflect upon the broader themes of spiritual warfare in the kingdom of God. However, the actual starting point should be to look at spiritual battles through the lens of the kingdom first, then through the lens of the church's mission next, and then through the lens of an individual Christian's life last. Yes, there are daily battles we need to combat that are happening inwardly within our hearts, but the battle between kingdoms is much greater than just one individual's plight.

In Colossians 3, the apostle Paul transitions us well from man's earthly battle against sin and flesh to the final battle that is to be secured by Jesus. He reminds those of us in Christ to seek the things above and stay focused on kingdom matters, not the things of this world. Hear what he says in Col 3:1–6.

---

6. Gen 3:1.

> [1] "If then you have been raised with Christ, seek the things that are above, where Christ is, seated at the right hand of God. [2] Set your minds on things that are above, not on things that are on earth. [3] For you have died, and your life is hidden with Christ in God. [4] When Christ who is your life appears, then you also will appear with him in glory.
> [5] Put to death therefore what is earthly in you: sexual immorality, impurity, passion, evil desire, and covetousness, which is idolatry. [6] On account of these the wrath of God is coming."

Whenever my sister died, I could only look at what happened through the lens of my own pain and loss. I felt like I had been robbed of something I held very dear, and I'm sure Satan would have loved for me to see it as a personal attack from God. I knew God could have healed my sister; we begged him to. But he didn't. He allowed the suffering even if he didn't cause it, and it would be easy to blame him for not intervening. Some days I did. But thankfully, God was patient with me in my doubts and questioning.

Now years later, I am able to look back at what happened through the kingdom lens and recognize that God was working something greater than my suffering. As I mentioned earlier in this book, two of my uncles, a cousin, and several friends of my sister placed their faith in Jesus at her funeral. When she took her last breath, I couldn't see at that moment a battle being fought for the kingdom of God and souls being won as a result of her death. Yes, I wish there could have been another way to their salvation without having to lose my best friend. But had Jaimie not died so young and tragically, I don't know if these people would have ever recognized their need for a Savior.

I cannot help but think of my sister's death in light of the verse that Joseph spoke to his brothers when he forgave them for selling him as a slave to Egypt, "As for you, you meant evil against me, but God meant it for good, to bring it about that many people should be kept alive, as they are today."[7] If I only look at Jaimie's death through the lens of what I lost personally, it's easy for me to be mad at God. But what the enemy meant for evil, God turned into good when those people were added to his kingdom the day we put her body to rest.

Not only that, but since my sister's death, I have been able to pour into countless others who are experiencing suffering and loss in my church and community by leading a GriefShare group alongside my parents and

---

7. Gen 50:20.

others. And had she not died, I would never have written this book, which is hopefully encouraging people all around the world to find hope amidst their own suffering, too. When I look through the kingdom lens at what I lost, I cannot help but give glory to God that the war against the enemy gained a little more ground that day, even though at the moment I thought I was losing. So remind yourself that whatever you are facing or suffering through right now, there is a bigger picture. It makes all the difference to have an eternal, kingdom-minded perspective.

There are kingdoms and principalities and demonic forces at war all around us every day that cannot be ignored. But if we are in Christ, we have no need to fear them, for the one more powerful than Satan is the one who created him—God. And if we are on his side, he is with us, holding us together and fighting on our behalf. Colossians 1:16–17 says:

> [16] For by him all things were created, in heaven and on earth, visible and invisible, whether thrones or dominions or rulers or authorities—all things were created through him and for him. [17] And he is before all things, and in him all things hold together.

God always has the final say. He will not allow anything to happen to you that doesn't go through him first. And we can trust he is working even the hardest situations for our good and his kingdom's glory. He has not left us alone to fight our battles. We do not have to rely on our own willpower and strength. So let's suit up with the armor of God, center our identity on Christ, and keep an eternal perspective when we face battles of any kind, whether internal battles of the heart, external battles of the world, or spiritual battles in the heavenly places. And as we fight, let's look toward the victory that is already secured for us in heaven. For Christ is promised to win. And God always keeps his promises.

Chapter Fourteen

Celebrating His Second Coming
The Battle of Waiting

Revelation 19:6–9

⁶ Then I heard what seemed to be the voice of a great multitude, like the roar of many waters and like the sound of mighty peals of thunder, crying out,

"Hallelujah!
For the Lord our God
the Almighty reigns.
⁷ Let us rejoice and exult
and give him the glory,
for the marriage of the Lamb has come,
and his Bride has made herself ready;
⁸ it was granted her to clothe herself
with fine linen, bright and pure"—

for the fine linen is the righteous deeds of the saints.

⁹ And the angel said to me, "Write this: Blessed are those who are invited to the marriage supper of the Lamb." And he said to me, "These are the true words of God."

CELEBRATING HIS SECOND COMING

Do you remember ever winning a ballgame or a contest as a kid and going out to celebrate with friends and family afterwards? Some of my fondest childhood memories revolve around playing little league baseball and celebrating afterwards with our parents and friends. Our team would practice so hard. We would play our best to battle against a strong opponent. And many times, we were victorious! But for those extra tough teams or championship games we won, we couldn't just high five and go home afterwards. Our victory merited a bigger celebration. We needed ice cream! So our parents would take us to Dairy Queen to celebrate the victory that had been won. And those were the times that victory never tasted so sweet *(literally)*!

But you know, an ice cream celebration pales in comparison to the victory celebration that is coming in the marriage supper of the Lamb. Back in the olden days, wedding parties could last days, even weeks, especially if it was a royal wedding (which is in this case with the King of kings)! People would feast for celebration, and people would feast when there was peace. That is what is happening in Revelation 19. Those who are redeemed by Jesus are invited to a great victory feast for all to share. And everyone at the table gets a heaping portion of the blessing.

There's a lot to say about Revelation that we are not able to cover in this book, but the more I study the first and second comings of Jesus, the more I realize that it doesn't matter when or how he comes. What matters is *that* he comes. And that we should be ready. But we do get glimpses of that day, of that final battle to end all battles, so for a moment, let's set our minds on things that are above. Let's take a quick look at that final battle in the Promised Land and note a few particulars from Revelation 19. This passage can be divided into three victorious parts. There is a victory hymn/song (1–5), a victory feast (6–10), and a victory battle (11–21).

Rejoicing in Heaven

> ¹After this I heard what seemed to be the loud voice of a great multitude in heaven, crying out,
>
> "Hallelujah!
> Salvation and glory and power belong to our God,
> ² for his judgments are true and just;
> for he has judged the great prostitute
>   who corrupted the earth with her immorality,
> and has avenged on her the blood of his servants."
>
> ³ Once more they cried out,

"Hallelujah!
The smoke from her goes up forever and ever."
⁴ And the twenty-four elders and the four living creatures fell down and worshiped God who was seated on the throne, saying, "Amen. Hallelujah!" ⁵ And from the throne came a voice saying,
"Praise our God,
all you his servants,
you who fear him,
small and great."[1]

The song sung in verses 1–5 are similar to victory hymns sung after a battle. What you hear is a celebratory song of victory and justice. A great multitude in heaven is crying out in praise that justice is fully and finally being delivered. And God, who is to be praised for the salvation and victory that he is bringing, is the one to be celebrated.

We don't have to wait until we get to heaven to join with this multitude and let the victories that God brings in our life turn into a beautifully loud sound glorifying God. Sometimes it's easy to get comfortable in our victories, no matter how big or small, and be tempted to take some of the credit. But don't forget God. Recognize what he has done in your life and praise him for it. In heaven there will be a multitude singing his praises because of what he's done for you and me. Let's join in the chorus now. It is God who reigns! It is God who is victorious! It is God who brings justice! Praise our God all you his servants.

The Marriage Supper of the Lamb

⁶ Then I heard what seemed to be the voice of a great multitude, like the roar of many waters and like the sound of mighty peals of thunder, crying out,

"Hallelujah!
For the Lord our God
the Almighty reigns.
⁷ Let us rejoice and exult
and give him the glory,
for the marriage of the Lamb has come,
and his Bride has made herself ready;
⁸ it was granted her to clothe herself
with fine linen, bright and pure"—

1. Rev 19:1–5.

for the fine linen is the righteous deeds of the saints.

⁹ And the angel said to me, "Write this: Blessed are those who are invited to the marriage supper of the Lamb." And he said to me, "These are the true words of God." ¹⁰ Then I fell down at his feet to worship him, but he said to me, "You must not do that! I am a fellow servant with you and your brothers who hold to the testimony of Jesus. Worship God." For the testimony of Jesus is the spirit of prophecy.[2]

Usually nations only sit down to feast when there is peace, and what we see in verses 6–10 is very similar to a victory feast after a war. This passage is reminiscent of Psalm 23, where the Good Shepherd prepares a table for us in the presence of our enemies.[3] But the order of celebration seems backwards in Revelation 19. You hear the hymn, see the feast, and then the final battle ensues. Why is that? Because the outcome of this battle is so certain that heaven celebrates the victory before it even happens! This gives us even greater assurance and hope to live amidst the *not yet* with the *already* in view. All of God's prophecies have come true before, so we know that what he says about the final battle will be true even before it happens. The battle has been won, so you can go ahead and celebrate!

The Rider on a White Horse

¹¹ Then I saw heaven opened, and behold, a white horse! The one sitting on it is called Faithful and True, and in righteousness he judges and makes war. ¹² His eyes are like a flame of fire, and on his head are many diadems, and he has a name written that no one knows but himself. ¹³ He is clothed in a robe dipped in blood, and the name by which he is called is The Word of God. ¹⁴ And the armies of heaven, arrayed in fine linen, white and pure, were following him on white horses. ¹⁵ From his mouth comes a sharp sword with which to strike down the nations, and he will rule them with a rod of iron. He will tread the winepress of the fury of the wrath of God the Almighty. ¹⁶ On his robe and on his thigh he has a name written, King of kings and Lord of lords.

¹⁷ Then I saw an angel standing in the sun, and with a loud voice he called to all the birds that fly directly overhead, "Come, gather for the great supper of God, ¹⁸ to eat the flesh of kings, the flesh of captains, the flesh of mighty men, the flesh of horses and

2. Rev 19:6–10.

3. Ps 23:5.

PART FOUR—JESUS THE CONQUERING KING

their riders, and the flesh of all men, both free and slave, both small and great." ¹⁹ And I saw the beast and the kings of the earth with their armies gathered to make war against him who was sitting on the horse and against his army. ²⁰ And the beast was captured, and with it the false prophet who in its presence had done the signs by which he deceived those who had received the mark of the beast and those who worshiped its image. These two were thrown alive into the lake of fire that burns with sulfur. ²¹ And the rest were slain by the sword that came from the mouth of him who was sitting on the horse, and all the birds were gorged with their flesh.[4]

In this last section of Revelation 19, Jesus shows up on the scene, now as the glorious king of the cosmos with a sword in his mouth and his robe dipped in the blood of all his enemies. Although the details seem a little weird in our minds now, we will not think it weird when we witness this some day. Nobody knows the day or the hour Jesus will return. No person. No angel. Not even the Son himself. What we do know is that he *is* going to return. And we know that it will be different from before. In his first coming, he came humbly to die in battle. In his second coming, he's coming in power to win the final battle. When we see Jesus on a horse with a sword in his mouth, we will know victory has been finally and fully won! Sin and Satan will be locked away forever.[5] V-day has come!

Anticipating the Wedding Day

Jesus is coming as a second Adam, restoring rulership over the new creation that is to come.[6] He will restore the Edenic *shalom* forfeited by the first Adam.[7] Dr. Phillip Bethancourt, a pastor and scholar in spiritual warfare, said, "The peace that the first Adam abandoned when he suffered the initial defeat of kingdom warfare is now restored by the second Adam who places all of his enemies under his feet at last.[8] With Christ's return, the new Eden that Israel failed to bring about in Canaan[9] will be established in the

---

4. Rev 19:11–21.
5. Revelation 20.
6. Rev 21:1–8.
7. Rev 21:3–4.
8. Rev 22:1–5.
9. Num 13:21–27.

new earth by the new Israel—Jesus himself."[10] Jesus is coming as a second Joshua and David as well, leading Israel into a new Jerusalem.[11] This new creation conquest will establish a new Promised Land in which the entire cosmos will be a land flowing with milk and honey.[12] The ways of Eden will be restored. And every day in heaven will be like one celebration after another forever and ever.

This concept of celebrating the marriage supper of the lamb is what fuels our hope every day and is worth waiting for. If you are married, you probably had a period of time between your engagement and the wedding day. Some had months. Others had years. But no matter how long of a time span, you were still engaged and committed during that time to the person whom you planned to marry. You were not married but your commitment was sure, usually backed by a ring and a promise of a future "Save the Date." In a similar way, Jesus's first coming is like the engagement party. For those who are in Christ, we have been sealed as if with an engagement ring, claiming his sacrifice on the cross for the forgiveness of our sins and believing that he will one day return to marry us. And when he comes again, the wedding will take place. We, the church—believers in Christ from all tribes and tongues and nations—are his bride. He, Christ Jesus, God in the flesh, is the groom. And he is coming back for us. We've got a wedding to get ready for!

I don't know about you, but waiting and anticipating my wedding day was hard, and I only had a six-month engagement. It did take me a couple of months to work up the courage to pop the question though, so I felt like in my heart it was longer. Waiting is hard. Anticipating something you want so bad when it seems so far off is even harder. But we must not give up and grow weary, leaving our groom at the alter without us. Because when the day finally comes, we will not think of all the grueling waiting we endured. We will just think of Jesus, and how glad we are to have him with us for the rest of our eternity. I love this encouragement the apostle Paul gives in Romans 8:

> [18] "For I consider that the sufferings of this present time are not worth comparing with the glory that is to be revealed to us. [19] For

---

10. I am indebted to Dr. Phillip Bethancourt for this material. Much of this information sprung from a conversation with him during the beginning stages of writing this book.

11. Rev 21:9–27.

12. Rev 22:1–5.

> the creation waits with eager longing for the revealing of the sons of God. [20] For the creation was subjected to futility, not willingly, but because of him who subjected it, in hope [21] that the creation itself will be set free from its bondage to corruption and obtain the freedom of the glory of the children of God. [22] For we know that the whole creation has been groaning together in the pains of childbirth until now. [23] And not only the creation, but we ourselves, who have the firstfruits of the Spirit, groan inwardly as we wait eagerly for adoption as sons, the redemption of our bodies. [24] For in this hope we were saved. Now hope that is seen is not hope. For who hopes for what he sees? [25] But if we hope for what we do not see, we wait for it with patience."[13]

For those already in Christ, we are secure in our engagement, and we know our fiancé is coming back for us. Therefore, we should want to be ready. We should want to look better than the world does and dress ourselves in purity and righteousness on the inside and out. We should want to please our future bridegroom. When he comes, we want him to look at us with love and joy in his eyes, saying "Well done. I am so glad you waited for me."

My wife and I waited to even kiss each other until our wedding day. We wanted to be pure for one another, but it didn't come without sacrifice. It was hard to resist that temptation many times and wait on something we couldn't yet see. But we wanted to honor each other, and more importantly, honor God's commands to be pure. And all those grueling years of saying "No" to temptations and opportunities that could have brought much temporary satisfaction to us were an afterthought on our wedding night when we finally could see that the wait had been worth it.

The Guest List

Yes, we may lament and groan while we anxiously await the day when the final battle will end all battles. When we will see a redemption of Eden and be given new bodies. When our hope of what we have *not yet* seen—Jesus—will be realized. But until that day, we must wait with patience. That's a hard word to practice, but it is necessary before we can partake in this ultimate wedding celebration that will go on and on forever. And while we

---

13. Rom 8:18–25.

wait, there is much to do. Like planning a wedding, you want to make sure everything's in place and all the guests are invited.

Jesus gave us a final battle plan right before he ascended into heaven on what we should do before he comes back again: "Go therefore and make disciples of all nations, baptizing them in the name of the Father and of the Son and of the Holy Spirit, teaching them to observe all that I have commanded you. And behold, I am with you always, to the end of the age."[14] The great commission to go into all the world and make disciples is not just a suggestion for Christians, it is a command. It is the siren call to commission the church to wage war and join Jesus in this battle of spiritual warfare. That can illuminate not just how we do church, but how we live day to day life.

All are invited to the marriage supper of the Lamb. All we have to do is accept the invitation. If you long for this place of perpetual peace, you still have time to attain it, but do not delay any longer in committing to this engagement today. It is a free gift given by the king of the cosmos with the promise to live abundantly in complete perfection forever. And all who are at the table will feast in peace forever and ever and ever.

This final battle ushers in our true Promised Land—abundant life forevermore. As you set your mind to these things that are above, let it fuel your fighting and waiting now. You don't have to wait until heaven to live a life of singing and feasting in the victory that is certain in Jesus. With God is always the victory. Every battle. Every time. But there's coming a day when there will be no more battles, and every sad and bad thing will come undone. This broken cosmos will be made new, from the furthest galaxy to your deepest heartache, because God has fought and won. He has always fought alongside his people. Let that fuel your hope. Let that fuel your waiting. Let that fuel your life. Jesus is worth waiting for. And when that day finally comes, the suffering we have endured now will be worth it.

---

14. Matt 28:19–20.

Chapter Fifteen

Pressing On with Forever in Mind
The Battle of Hope

---

2 Corinthians 4:16–18

[16] So we do not lose heart. Though our outer self is wasting away, our inner self is being renewed day by day. [17] For this light momentary affliction is preparing for us an eternal weight of glory beyond all comparison, [18] as we look not to the things that are seen but to the things that are unseen. For the things that are seen are transient [fleeting], but the things that are unseen are eternal.

I DON'T KNOW ANYBODY who likes getting shots. If you think about it, there is initially no good reason why someone would willingly pay a doctor money to stab you with a piece of metal and pump a foreign substance into your body, leaving you sore for days and maybe even emotionally traumatized, especially if you're a kid. And no, I'm not here to engage in a debate about vaccines and their safety. I'm just trying to use an analogy for this chapter's purpose, so bear with me.

Despite all the bad rap that vaccines get, many people get shots on a yearly, monthly, and even daily basis. Some people get shots voluntarily to avoid catching a sickness, like the flu, but others have little to no choice whether to get them or not when they are essential for fighting terminal diseases, like tetanus or diabetes. I get a shot every few years or so, but it doesn't matter how long it has been since my last one, anytime I'm about to be poked, I have to psych myself out for it. I'm not one of the weird people who likes to watch the needle go in. In fact, I usually turn my head the other way and pinch myself with my other hand to counteract the pain and trick my brain into focusing on the pinch instead.

Imagine if the pain of shots lasted minutes, even hours. And it wasn't a quick stick, inject, and pull-out process. No. It was a rapid-fire poke, poke, poke, inject, then twist, twist, twist, then repeat the process multiple times with nothing to numb the pain. I'm cringing just thinking about it. If that's how vaccines worked, I'm certain I would rather just get sick. Or imagine if shots were for no good purpose, but they were trendy and fun and you could pick your own style—scented, sparkly, extra-long needles if you prefer a little more excitement. Mix and match how you like it. Everyone's doing it. But there are no health benefits. It's just for the thrill and excitement to see how tough you are. Kind of like riding roller coasters but in a much more painful way. How do you think the public would react? Would people go out of their way and spend tons of money for these gratuitous vaccines? No way! Those clinics would close down quicker than a frozen yogurt shop at Christmas.

But here's the deal. We do get shots. We do pay people to stick us. We do go out of our way and even hold down our screaming children for them sometimes. Why? Because the pain is temporary and often for good purposes. It's the same way that hoping in heaven helps us persevere through life on earth. You can endure the pain of receiving a shot because you know the pain is temporary and the present discomfort is working something good within you. It makes the current pain more bearable. That is how we should think of evil and suffering in this life in light of eternity. It is working something good in us, whether it be the fruits of the Spirit or union with Christ. Maybe our suffering is pointing someone else to Jesus who wouldn't see him otherwise. Or maybe it is working in us our dependency on Christ and not ourselves, teaching us to find satisfaction in him alone. Whatever it is working, no matter how painful it may be, it is a light and momentary affliction compared to the glory that awaits us.[1]

But what if our suffering has lasted our whole life? What if the pain is so intense it is barely bearable? How can Paul say our afflictions are light

---

1. 2 Cor 4:17.

and momentary? He doesn't know what has happened to me! But even if he did know, I'm certain Paul would still say the same thing, no matter what the situation is. You may not see your suffering as light and momentary right now. But a million years from now it will be as if it didn't exist.

Do you remember the shot you got when you were five or six years old? I remember a few years ago having to hold down my son at that age along with another nurse's help while yet another nurse gave him the shot. He has a fight or flight response anytime he is overwhelmed with fear, and that day he was scared. He didn't have the capacity to rationalize in that moment that the pain would only last half a second. If he did, it would have helped him persevere through the discomfort. But he was screaming and thrashing so bad that when they finally did stick him, he didn't even realize it until the nurse said, "It's over." And ten years from now, he won't even remember that day, even though it was unbearable for him (and me!).

When you live with the realization that an eternity of no more suffering awaits those who are in Christ, it allows you to persevere through even a lifetime of suffering here on earth. Hope for a time when it will not hurt, like a shot, is what allows us to persevere and keep going through the pain now. And not only can we see our suffering as temporary when we have hope of better days, but also we can see it as good. Even if you can't see the good of your suffering now or ever in this life, you can agree with the apostle Paul, who knew suffering very well, that it is preparing for you an eternal weight of glory beyond all comparison. You don't have to see the good now to know that God is working a good that will last forever. Remember that kingdom-minded perspective we talked about earlier? Having an eternal perspective allows you to persevere through any hardship you may be experiencing now.

Death to Death

What Paul says in 1 Corinthians 15 is helpful in understanding this eternal perspective of suffering. It centers our reality on the reality of the resurrection of Jesus, as we discussed in chapter 10. And the resurrection of Jesus reminds us that death was not only defeated for Jesus, but it is defeated for us as well. I encourage you to read the entire chapter of 1 Corinthians 15 for yourself *(please do read it; don't simply glance past it)*, but let's look at this particular passage that gives me great hope:

> ⁵⁴ "When the perishable puts on the imperishable, and the mortal puts on immortality, then shall come to pass the saying that is written:
>
>> "Death is swallowed up in victory."
>> ⁵⁵ "O death, where is your victory?
>> O death, where is your sting?"
>
> ⁵⁶ The sting of death is sin, and the power of sin is the law. ⁵⁷ But thanks be to God, who gives us the victory through our Lord Jesus Christ."[2]

There is coming a day when death will die. Hallelujah! Remember when we discussed earlier that the kingdom of God is both *already* and *not yet*? Well there is coming a day when the *not yet* becomes the *already*. Because of that, throughout the history and flow of Scripture and the kingdoms and the battles in between, there is hope. There is hope in the *not yet* because the *yet* remains, and the *yet* is sure. The *yet* is the restoration of all things. It is the defeating of all of our worst enemies. It is death to death. It was all purchased by Jesus, and it is going to be fulfilled by Jesus. He is both the Slaughtered Lamb and the Conquering King. His kingdom, as promised long ago, will have no end. The Lion of the tribe of Judah will reign forever and ever, and all bad things will come to an end.

No More Hope

Not only will all bad things come to an end, but hope will come to an end, too. *Wait, what?* Isn't hope a good thing? Yes, and heaven will be full of all good things. But once we get there, we will have no more need to hope because our hope will be established when we stand before the One in whom our hope is placed. While we are here on earth, we hope because we do not yet see the fulfillment of the promise. We await its glorious arrival. We long for the day, "till there's no more faith and no more hope; I'll see your face and Lord I'll know," as Andrew Peterson sings in his song "No More Faith."

In heaven, there will be no need for faith or hope because faith will be actualized and hope will be established. Hope is what drives us forward, and faith is what makes our hope certain. "So now faith, hope, and love abide, these three; but the greatest of these is love."[3] Love, the love of God,

---

2. 1 Cor 15:54–56.
3. 1 Cor 13:13.

is what propels us to hope in him and is what will remain when hope and faith both fade into obscurity. When we see Jesus face to face, there will be no more hope, no more faith, and no more pain. Only love will remain. And oh, I can't wait for that day!

Since losing my twin sister, I find myself saying often to people going through hardships, "Our hope is in heaven." It means that Jaimie is waiting for me. Yet even better than Jaimie waiting to greet me when I die is Jesus waiting for me. He is preparing a place for us.[4] A place with no more mourning. No more pain. No more death. There will be only happy thoughts and awestricken moments, and if there are any tears at all, they will only be the good kind that come from laughing too hard or realizing that something is a little too beautiful for words. Placing our hope in heaven means that though we suffer here on earth, we don't have to sit in our suffering forever. It means we can get up and walk forward, even if it is with a limp. It means that though we may never sprint in this life again, one day we will soar with wings like eagles.[5] Heavenly hope is the vehicle by which the sufferer travels within and through this abundant Christian life, until our hope is finally actualized.

I cling to this promise of what is to come in Rev 21:3–5:

> [3] And I heard a loud voice from the throne saying, "Behold, the dwelling place of God is with man. He will dwell with them, and they will be his people, and God himself will be with them as their God. [4] He will wipe away every tear from their eyes, and death shall be no more, neither shall there be mourning, nor crying, nor pain anymore, for the former things have passed away. And he who was seated on the throne said, "Behold, I am making all things new."

God's plan all along has been to mend what was broken in the garden of Eden and return us to a walking, talking relationship with him in a land where he is making all things new. We will dwell with God again and he will be our satisfaction and joy. We will no longer deal with temptation and depression and addiction and the constant need for approval and the desire for more and fractured relationships and broken marriages and wayward children and the numbing loss of a loved one and doubts and fears and gossip and speeding tickets and fractured fellowship over petty things and making big deals out of little things and a myriad of other harmful, frustrating, painful, no-good things. One day, everything that has caused us

---

4. John 14:2–3.
5. Isa 40:31.

hardship in this life will be washed away by the blood of the Lamb, just as our sins are.[6] It has been promised. And God always keeps his promises.

Hope is a powerful thing. It helps us to keep going through these light and momentary afflictions. It reminds us that God is bigger than our situation; that he is with us even to the end of the age.[7] And even though we should continue fighting for hope in a world that is becoming more and more hopeless, one day our battle of hope will end. We won't need to hang onto it anymore because it will be standing in front of us in the person of Jesus. Let the *not yet* fuel your *already*, and "press on toward the goal for the prize of the upward call of God in Christ Jesus."[8]

---

6. Isa 1:18.
7. Matt 28:20.
8. Phil 3:14.

Chapter Sixteen

Comprehending the Greatest of Loves
The Battle is No More

---

1 John 4:13–18

[13] By this we know that we abide in him and he in us, because he has given us of his Spirit. [14] And we have seen and testify that the Father has sent his Son to be the Savior of the world. [15] Whoever confesses that Jesus is the Son of God, God abides in him, and he in God. [16] So we have come to know and to believe the love that God has for us. God is love, and whoever abides in love abides in God, and God abides in him. [17] By this is love perfected with us, so that we may have confidence for the day of judgment, because as he is so also are we in this world.

IF YOU HAVE MADE it this far, thank you for sticking out a very hard and heavy book. No one would choose to willingly read about suffering unless you have in some way or another been affected by it in this world. Which we all have. But if you are in Christ, I hope you have been encouraged in your suffering and reminded of God's goodness and faithfulness throughout all history. And if you are still skeptical to the hope he offers, I hope this final chapter solidifies the truth of the gospel in your heart.

Many people deny God's goodness because of evil and suffering in this world. They think, "If God was loving and good, why would he allow such evil and suffering to exist?" Maybe you are one who has asked that question because bad things happened to you, bad things happened to your parents, or bad things happened to your grandparents, and the list goes on and on. While that is a valid question that many people have, and one that I will seek to answer in this chapter, it is incredibly farsighted. It looks far into the past of what God didn't do, yet fails to see in the moment what he is doing right now in front of you. His goodness, his love, his salvation, and his sovereignty are real and do not contradict each other, no matter how much evil and suffering you or others before you have experienced in this life.

When we deny God because of past experiences, whether our own or not, it's like being mad every day since you were three that you were thirsty and didn't have water, even though there is a pitcher of water sitting right in front of you now. The incredible thing is not the thousands of years that suffering and evil have existed. The incredible thing is that God's plan, from before the creation of the world, was for himself to be the sacrifice that atones for the evil and sins of all the people, purchasing a literal forever with no more evil and suffering. Did I mention *forever*? Not only do you have a pitcher of water in front of you now, but it's as if somehow, all the thirst you've ever experienced throughout your entire life has made it possible for you to one day never be thirsty again. Forever.

Analogies only go so far, but hopefully you see my point. I think it's important to point out that thirst—in this analogy, referring to evil and suffering—must exist because we are human and our bodies require water, just as if we are truly free, evil and suffering have to be possible. Not just for freedom's sake, but for love's sake in order for us to be able to truly comprehend love.

The Greatest of Goods

The greatest of goods that has ever existed is love. And as was discussed in the previous chapter, out of faith, hope and love, love alone will remain and is the greatest of the three. Love, in many forms, drives all our actions and our life's pursuits. But what is love? How do we know when we are truly experiencing it? John 15:13 states, "Greater love has no one than this, that someone lay down his life for his friends." And there is someone who has laid down his life for you—Jesus.

Without sacrifice of some sort, there is no possibility for truly knowing and experiencing love. If we were created as robots, not able to make real choices on our own, we could never have the capacity or even the category of thought to know what love is. We would be in an endless cycle of robotic determinism. But God decided to create the world with free creatures who could act on good or evil, knowing that evil was a possibility in his good and perfect creation. He created us knowing that man would sin, but also knowing that he himself would be the sacrifice for our sin. That was the only way humanity could comprehend the greatest of loves and God could demonstrate that love.

Here is where skeptics get nearsighted, while previously being farsighted (I guess it is clinical blindness now), therefore missing the point and not seeing the awe and wonder and glory and goodness that is shouting so loudly right at them. In Jesus, we get to know and experience the greatest of loves for all eternity. God created us in such a way where we couldn't live in a sinless world, but we could partake in a sinless eternity where only love —the greatest of goods—remains.

This is the greatest mystery of all. The mystery into which angels long to look.[1] This is the good news that is to be proclaimed to the ends of the earth.[2] That you can have an eternity of no evil. *Forever.* All the evil that has ever existed when measured against the pure goodness that is offered through Jesus for all eternity will be so minuscule it will be invisible. As Frederick Buechner poignantly said in his novel *Godric*, "All the death that ever was, set next to life, would scarcely fill a cup." When Jesus comes to make all things new, evil and suffering will be so far in the past that the Hubble telescope won't even be able to see it.

Elisabeth Elliot makes a good point to combat skepticism by saying, "We would never ask the question why if we really believed that the whole of the universe was an accident and that you and I are completely at the mercy of chance."[3] Later, she goes on to say, "God, through my own troubles and sufferings, has not given me explanations. But he has met me as a person, as an individual, and that's what we need."[4] Even when we don't get answers as to why bad things have happened to us, we can know that God has been and always will be good, and he's working all things for good, even evil.

1. 1 Pet 1:12.
2. Luke 2:10–11; Matt 28:19–20; Acts 1:8.
3. Elliot, *Suffering Is Never for Nothing*, 21.
4. Elliot, *Suffering Is Never for Nothing*, 23.

O Felix Culpa

I first came across the concept that God purposed a world with evil and suffering to bring about greater goods through the famed Christian philosopher Alvin Plantinga. He has been at the forefront of the debate of what's called "the problem of evil" for half a century. Decades ago, his free will defense essentially singlehandedly hushed the voices that said that there is a contradiction between the omni-attributes of God (being all-powerful, all-knowing, and all-good) and the existence of evil and suffering. And maybe you struggle with that question, too: "If a good God exists, then why is there evil?" From Epicurus to David Hume and beyond, it was argued that if evil and suffering exists, then God is neither all-powerful, nor all-good, or he flat-out doesn't exist.

Plantinga offered a possible explanation to that question. He brought it back to creation and explained that God, in his infinite knowledge and power, could design any world he wanted to before he decided to create. And suppose that of all the worlds God could create, he knew the best possible one was the one in which free creatures existed. Creatures that could make decisions on their own. So God, being infinite in goodness, chose to create the best of possible worlds, and he did. But here's the catch. For the best of possible worlds to have free creatures, it would also have to have the possibility of evil and suffering.

If creatures have free choices, you cannot force them to choose good every time. We see that with Adam and Eve. They were free to choose from every tree in the garden except for the tree of the knowledge of good and evil (Gen 2:15–17). And they freely chose evil. In this possible scenario that Plantinga presented, God is still all-good, all-knowing, and all-powerful, yet evil and suffering still exist. But there is no contradiction in his character. And you might say, "Well why couldn't God have just made a world without evil?" Because without evil how would we know what is good? We would just be going through the motions, no good and no bad, no highs and no lows, just continual mundane existence. We wouldn't know evil, but we also wouldn't know good. That scenario, in my opinion, is more evil than the one we live in where suffering and evil exists.

After decades of championing *possible* solutions (which are called defenses) of a good God allowing evil and downplaying the effectiveness of more certain solutions (which are called theodicies), Plantinga proposed his own theodicy. He called it *O Felix Culpa*, which is Latin for "fortunate fall" or "happy fault." *Felix culpa* arguments in general have a long history.

Arthur O. Lovejoy dates the phrase to originate with either Gregory the Great (540–604) or the Roman Catholic Easter liturgy, *Exultet*, in his evaluation of its usage within Milton's *Paradise Lost*, which itself dates to 1667.[5] It is precisely from the Easter liturgy, *Exultet*, that Plantinga derived the name for his theodicy, O *Felix Culpa*.[6]

The idea inherent within the phrase O *Felix Culpa* is that the boundless blessing of knowing God's love through the incarnation and atonement of Christ would not exist apart from the existence of sin and evil.[7] The incarnation is God taking on flesh in the person of Jesus. The atonement is Jesus dying as the once-for-all sacrifice for the sins of all who believe. There is no need for atonement without something that needs atoning. Evil must exist if atonement exists. And the incarnation exists to provide atonement because it requires God himself dying in the place of man.

Gottfried W. Leibniz reveals this notion, stating, "The ancients called Adam's fall *Felix Culpa*, a happy sin, because it had been retrieved with immense advantage by the incarnation of the Son of God, who has given to the universe something nobler than anything that ever would have been among creatures except for this."[8] Meaning, without sin ever entering into the world, we would not have a complete picture of how far the love of God would go for us. Remember the verse I mentioned earlier in chapter 13, *"As for you, you meant evil against me, but God meant it for good, to bring it about that many people should be kept alive, as they are today"*?[9] Plantinga's theodicy specifically argues that the incarnation and atonement of Jesus are *infinite goods* that came out of the fall (evil), and any world without incarnation and atonement would be less good.[10]

But how are the incarnation and atonement infinite goods? How do they solve the problem of evil and suffering? And how are non-Christians to view it as an answer to why evil and suffering exists? It all boils down, once again, to love. God could have created us as deterministic robots, unable to make free decisions, yet submitting to his every wish and command. Sort of like puppets on a string. But just as Pinocchio wanted to be a real boy and come and go as he pleased, God knew if he forced us to only be good

---

5. Lovejoy, "Milton and the Paradox of the Fortunate Fall," 169.
6. Plantinga, "Supralapsarianism, or 'O Felix Culpa,'" 12n17.
7. Weisinger, *Tragedy and the Paradox of the Fortunate Fall*, 19.
8. Leibniz, *Philosophical Works of Leibniz*, 194–5.
9. Gen 50:20.
10. Plantinga, "Supralapsarianism, or 'O Felix Culpa,'" 10.

COMPREHENDING THE GREATEST OF LOVES

and choose good, we would lack a comprehension of real love. It wouldn't be a two-way street. So God created humans with free will in order for us to have the capacity to love and be loved. Just as you cannot give something you do not yet have, love first comes from God, because he is love. 1 John 4:7–10 says:

> [7] Beloved, let us love one another, for love is from God, and whoever loves has been born of God and knows God. [8] Anyone who does not love does not know God, because God is love. [9] In this the love of God was made manifest among us, that God sent his only Son into the world, so that we might live through him. [10] In this is love, not that we have loved God but that he loved us and sent his Son to be the propitiation for our sins.

God does not need our love to fulfill himself, although he probably enjoys it just like any good father whose children love and respect him would. But he didn't create us in order for us to love him. God created us to display his glory to the world through his love. We see this in Isa 43:6–7 when God says, "bring my sons from afar and my daughters from the end of the earth, everyone who is called by my name, whom I created for my glory, whom I formed and made." He created us with the capacity to freely choose good or evil so that we could freely know love. Some say we wouldn't be able to love at all if we didn't have free will, though that is debated.[11] But that's not what I'm saying here, even if it is true. What I am saying is without the ability to freely act, we wouldn't have the capability to comprehend love. And ultimately, without the incarnation and atonement (God taking on flesh to die in the place of our sins), we wouldn't be able to comprehend the greatest of loves. Part of the infinite goods of the incarnation and atonement are not that they are good by nature, but that they are good *forever*. The redeemed will be able to fully comprehend the greatest of loves for all eternity, which wouldn't be possible without the Fall into sin. *O Felix Culpa*, indeed.

Comprehending Love

How do you know somebody loves you? Is it through their words? If they say, "I love you," do you believe them? They may just be saying it and not truly mean it. What if they do something for you? They could just be doing something in order to get something in return. There might not be actual

---

11. Williams, *God Reforms Hearts*.

love behind it, or they might simply be going through the motions. We in our sinful nature are automatically selfish. So even our most noble acts of love can be self-serving. The only way you can truly know someone loves you is by their other-centered self-sacrifice. If their actions show their love without expecting anything in return, and actually to their own detriment, you can know they love you.

Have you ever heard the phrase, "Love hurts"? There are lots of takes on that (and even a few songs), but I'm not talking about the heartbreak of loving someone who doesn't love you in return. I'm talking about the crazy things you endure to be with someone you love. You cross oceans for them, lose sleep over them, spend all your money on them, give up your time for them. You sacrifice your own desires to put their wants above yours. You give up things for them that you never thought you could live without. You would even die for them if you had to. You would be willing to sacrifice and hurt in order to show that person you would go to any lengths for them. You can know someone loves you when they have this kind of other-centered self-sacrifice.

There is no greater other-centered act than self-sacrifice. Gene H. Outka, an expert on *agape* (which is the biblical, no-strings-attached type love), argues, "In a world of vying interests the purest expression of agape becomes self-sacrifice."[12] The highest ideals of love are always expressed through self-sacrifice. The Good Samaritan sacrificed his time, energy, money, and reputation.[13] The Good Shepherd sacrificed his life when he laid it down for his sheep.[14] Self-sacrificial love is the greatest expression of love, as evidenced from the Scriptures. It is how we know real love and should model it after Jesus.[15]

Love Forevermore

In theological terms, eschatology is the term used when considering last things (like end times or heaven and hell), which has been our focus in this final section. Because of Jesus's love for us, we can have eschatological hope. In Revelation 5, we see a prophecy of Jesus coming on the scene in heaven amidst intense weeping because no one is found worthy to break the seal

---

12. Outka, *Agape*, 169.
13. Luke 10:25–37.
14. John 10:11.
15. John 15:13.

COMPREHENDING THE GREATEST OF LOVES

and open the scrolls of God's judgment.[16] It seems like sin will continue to reign, which in my mind is a good reason to weep uncontrollably because that is the result of evil and suffering. But one of the elders says to John, the writer of Revelation, "Weep no more; behold, the Lion of the tribe of Judah, the Root of David, has conquered, so that he can open the scroll and its seven seals."[17] Then John looks up and sees Jesus as a lamb that has been slain.[18]

Even though Jesus is in heaven, he displays the evidence of his earthly sacrifice. Why? Because Jesus is the image of love, and true love requires sacrifice.[19] Before John ever had this vision on the Island of Patmos, he had written this statement in one of his letters, "By this we know love, that he laid down his life for us."[20] Before the resurrected Jesus[21] ascended into heaven, he revealed himself to his disciples, and they saw his scars where the nails pierced his hands. For many of them, it was touching and seeing his scars that removed their doubts that it was really him. Jesus was miraculously whole and healed in every other way except for his scars, I think to forever show his sacrifice of love.

One day, Jesus will make all things new. He will bring about the ultimate restoration and redemption of all things. Though evil and suffering exists in the here and now, and it hurts, there is coming a day when evil and suffering will be no more, and only love, the greatest good, will remain. Faith and hope are incredible goods that get us through this life, but we won't need them in heaven. Only love will remain.[22] Love is the one thing that will never end.

Because of the sacrifice of Jesus, we can fully comprehend the greatest of loves forever and ever. And because of Jesus, our tears can be wiped away for he is worthy to open the scroll. That certainly is the greatest of goods. That makes all the suffering up to this point fade into obscurity amidst an eternity of unbounded love. Not only do those who are redeemed on earth recognize for themselves the love God has for them, but they are able to fully comprehend the greatest of loves forever in heaven because the

16. Rev 5:4.
17. Rev 5:5.
18. Rev 5:6.
19. 1 John 4:7.
20. 1 John 3:16.
21. Haywood, *Felix Culpa...Christus Resurrexit*.
22. 1 Cor 13:8, 13.

PART FOUR—JESUS THE CONQUERING KING

self-sacrificial expression of God's love on the cross will fully be on display. This reality affects everything, both presently and forever, on earth as it is in heaven.

There will be a day when the final battle will be over, and only love will remain. The result will be a new Promised Land, a heavenly city unlike anything we have ever experienced on earth. It will be a land with no temple or church, because forever the *tabernacle* or dwelling place of God will be with man.[23] It will be a land with no sun or moon[24] because the radiance of the glory of Christ—the light that has been shining amidst our darkness—will illuminate all the cosmos with the darkness never overcoming it. It will be a land with no night because Jesus, the light, will be present with us at all times.[25] It will be a land with no closed gates because there will be no need for protection.[26] Every enemy will have been defeated and locked away forever,[27] so there will be nothing to fear. Safety will be sure. Peace will abound forevermore. It will be a land with no need for worry or doubt or any coping mechanism that we have become so accustomed to in our daily lives because there will be no more battles. It will be a land with no need for rest because we will be in perfected bodies amidst perpetual rest.[28] It will be a land with no more death, which means there will be no mourning or crying or pain.[29] It will be a land with no more sin because nothing unclean can enter it.[30] Only those who names are written in the Lamb's book of life. And most importantly, it will be a land where our Lord and Savior Jesus Christ is. The long-awaited Messiah. The Slaughtered Lamb. The Conquering King. The only one worthy to open the scroll. The only one who can defeat sin and death. The only way to this everlasting Promised Land. He is the ultimate representation of love, and therefore, he will remain and reign forevermore.

Dear reader, I hope to see you someday in the new and perfect Promised Land, where every struggle we ever fought in this life will be forgotten in the face of unending love. Until we meet again, may you continue to

23. Rev 21:22.
24. Rev 21:23.
25. Rev 21:25.
26. Rev 21:25.
27. Rev 20:10.
28. Phil 3:21; Heb 4:9–11.
29. Rev 21:4.
30. Rev 21:27.

"fight the good fight"[31] and "run with endurance the race that is set before [you], looking to Jesus, the founder and perfecter of [your] faith."[32] Keep the faith, cling to hope, walk in love. There is abundance of life waiting for you.

---

31. 1 Tim 6:12.
32. Heb 12:1–2.

Bibliography

"11 Reasons Spurgeon Was Depressed." *The Spurgeon Center*, July 11, 2017. https://www.spurgeon.org/resource-library/blog-entries/11-reasons-spurgeon-was-depressed.

Baker, Frank, ed. *Representative Verse of Charles Wesley*. Vancouver, BC: Regent College Publishing, 2022.

Boice, James Montgomery. *Joshua: An Expositional Commentary*. Grand Rapids: Baker, 1989.

Briones, David. "Already, Not Yet: How to Live in the Last Days." *Desiring God*. https://www.desiringgod.org/articles/already-not-yet.

Carson, D.A. *Holy Sonnets of the Twentieth Century*. Grand Rapids: Baker, 1994.

Claypool, John R. *Tracks of a Fellow Struggler*. New York: Word, 1974.

Davies, Horton. *The Communion of Saints: Prayers of the Famous*. Grand Rapids: Eerdmans, 1996.

Dawkins, Richard. *River Out of Eden: A Darwinian View of Life*. New York: Basic, 1995.

Doyle, Arthur Conan. *A Study in Scarlet*. Project Gutenberg. https://www.gutenberg.org/files/244/244-h/244-h.htm.

Ehrman, Bart D. *The New Testament: A Historical Introduction to the Early Christian Writings*. New York: Oxford University Press, 2011.

Elliot, Elisabeth. *Suffering Is Never for Nothing*. Nashville: B&H, 2019.

Got Questions. "What is the concept of 'already not yet'?" https://www.gotquestions.org/already-not-yet.html.

Groothuis, Douglas. *Walking Through Twilight: A Wife's Illness-A Philosopher's Lament*. Downers Grove, IL: InterVarsity, 2017.

Guthrie, Nancy. *Holding On to Hope: A Pathway through Suffering to the Heart of God*. Carol Stream, IL: Tyndale Momentum, 2015.

Habermas, Gary. "Ancient Non-Christian Sources." *LBTS Faculty Publications and Presentations* (1996). https://digitalcommons.liberty.edu/cgi/viewcontent.cgi?article=1038&context=lts_fac_pubs.

Haywood, Jacob H. "*Felix Culpa...Christus Resurrexit*: Resurrection and Plantinga's Infinite Goods." *Journal of the Evangelical Theological Society* 66.2 (2023) 315–22.

Huston, Katy Bowser. *Now I Lay Me Down to Fight*. Downers Grove, IL: IVP, 2023.

Interlandi, Jeneen. "New Estimate Boosts the Human Brain's Memory Capacity 10-Fold." *Scientific American*, February 5, 2016. https://www.scientificamerican.com/article/new-estimate-boosts-the-human-brain-s-memory-capacity-10-fold/.

BIBLIOGRAPHY

"It Is Well With My Soul." *Spafford Hymn.org.* https://www.spaffordhymn.com.

Josephus. "The Life of Flavius Josephus." *Perseus Digital Library.* https://www.perseus.tufts.edu/hopper/text?doc=Perseus%3Atext%3A1999.01.0150%3Asection%3D414.

Keller, W. Phillip. *Joshua: Man of Fearless Faith.* Waco, TX: Word, 1983.

Leibniz, Gottfried W. *The Philosophical Works of Leibnitz.* Translated by George M. Duncan. New Haven, CT: Tuttle, Morehouse & Taylor, 1890.

Letham, R. W. A. "Incarnation." In *New Dictionary of Theology,* edited by Sinclair B. Ferguson, David F. Wright, J.I. Packer, 333–35. Downers Grove, IL: IVP Academic, 1988.

Lewis, C.S. *Miracles.* San Francisco, CA: HarperOne, 2015.

Licona, Michael R. *The Resurrection of Jesus: A New Historiographical Approach.* Downers Grove, IL: InterVarsity, 2010.

Ligonier Ministries. "A Man After God's Own Heart." November 20, 2008. https://www.ligonier.org/blog/a-man-after-gods-own-heart.

Lovejoy, Arthur O. "Milton and the Paradox of the Fortunate Fall." *ELH* 4, no. 3 (1937): 161–79.

McGee, J. Vernon. *Joshua and Judges.* Nashville, TN: Thomas Nelson, 1991.

McKinley, David. "The Significance of the Psalms for Spurgeon." *The Spurgeon Center,* November 2, 2021. https://www.spurgeon.org/resource-library/blog-entries/the-significances-of-the-psalms-for-spurgeon.

Merida, Tony. *Exalting Jesus in Acts.* Christ-Centered Exposition Commentary. Nashville: B&H, 2017.

Meyer, Don. "I Heard the Bells on Christmas Day." *HuffPost,* December 17, 2012. https://www.huffpost.com/entry/i-heard-the-bells-on-chri_b_2316476.

Nouwen, Henri J.M. *A Letter of Consolation.* San Francisco: HarperSanFrancisco, 1982.

Outka, Gene H. *Agape: An Ethical Analysis.* New Haven: Yale University Press, 1972.

Pascal, Blaise. "Prayer, to Ask of God the Proper Use of Sickness." *Bartlby.* https://web.archive.org/web/20100217071055/http://bartleby.com/48/3/2.html.

Plantinga, Alvin. "Supralapsarianism, or 'O Felix Culpa.'" In *Christian Faith and the Problem of Evil,* edited by Peter Van Inwagen, 1–25. Grand Rapids: William B. Eerdmans, 2004.

Ray, Charles. "The Life of Susannah Spurgeon." In *Morning Devotions by Susannah Spurgeon: Free Grace and Dying Love.* Edinburgh: Banner of Truth, 2006.

Reeves, Michael. "Did You Know That Charles Spurgeon Struggled With Depression?" *Crossway,* February 24, 2018. https://www.crossway.org/articles/did-you-know-that-charles-spurgeon-struggled-with-depression.

Schaeffer, Francis A. *Joshua and the Flow of Biblical History.* Wheaton, IL: Crossway, 2004.

———. *True Spirituality.* Carol Stream, IL: Tyndale, 1971.

Schreiner, Thomas R. *Galatians.* Exegetical Commentary on the New Testament. Grand Rapids: Zondervan, 2010.

Spurgeon, C.H. *The Metropolitan Tabernacle Pulpit Sermons.* 63 vols. London: Passmore & Alabaster, 1855–1917.

———. "Psalm 3." *The Spurgeon Archive.* https://archive.spurgeon.org/treasury/ps003.php.

———. "Psalm 18." *The Spurgeon Archive.* https://archive.spurgeon.org/treasury/ps018.php.

———. "Psalm 30." *The Spurgeon Archive.* https://archive.spurgeon.org/treasury/ps030.php

———. "Psalm 34." *The Spurgeon Archive.* https://archive.spurgeon.org/treasury/ps034.php.

———. "Psalm 57." *The Spurgeon Archive.* https://archive.spurgeon.org/treasury/ps057.php.

———. "Psalm 59." *The Spurgeon Archive.* https://archive.spurgeon.org/treasury/ps059.php https://archive.spurgeon.org/treasury/ps059.php.

———. "Psalm 63." *The Spurgeon Archive.* https://archive.spurgeon.org/treasury/ps063.php.

———. "Psalm 136." *The Spurgeon Archive.* https://archive.spurgeon.org/treasury/ps136.php.

Taylor, Justin. "The True Story of Pain and Hope Behind 'I Heard the Bells on Christmas Day.'" *The Gospel Coalition,* December 21, 2014. https://www.thegospelcoalition.org/blogs/justin-taylor/the-story-of-pain-and-hope-behind-i-heard-the-bells-on-christmas-day/.

Tileston, Mary W., ed. *Great Souls at Prayer.* London: Pitman, 1963.

Vroegop, Mark. *Dark Clouds, Deep Mercy: Discovering the Grace of Lament.* Wheaton, IL: Crossway, 2019.

Weisinger, Herbert. *Tragedy and the Paradox of the Fortunate Fall.* London: Routledge & Kegan Paul Ltd, 1953.

White, R. E. O. "Sanctification." In *Evangelical Dictionary of Theology,* edited by Daniel J. Treier and Walter A. Elwell, 770–72. Grand Rapids: Baker Academic, 2017.

Wiersbe, Warren W. *The Wiersbe Bible Commentary: Old Testament.* Colorado Springs: David C. Cook, 2007.

Williams, Thaddeus. *God Reforms Hearts: Rethinking Free Will and the Problem of Evil.* Bellingham, WA: Lexham Academic, 2021.

Wilson, Gerald H. *Psalms Volume 1.* The NIV Application Commentary. Grand Rapids: Zondervan, 2002.

Wolterstorff, Nicholas. *Lament for a Son.* Grand Rapids: Eerdmans, 1987.

Wright, N. T. *The Resurrection of the Son of God.* Minneapolis: Fortress, 2003.